cupcakes
& fairycakes

THE AUSTRALIAN
Women's Weekly

contents

These exquisite little cakes are ideal for afternoon tea, as an elegant and chic dessert for a dinner party, or as a splendid and original birthday cake. While it's true they look like little works of art, and a few of them require some cake decorating experience, most of them are not difficult to make. *The Australian Women's Weekly* Test Kitchen team has had the best fun dreaming up ideas for the design of these little masterpieces, and playing with the flavours so they complement the look of the cakes.

Pamela Clark

Food Director

veryberry cakes

Dried berry buttercake

125g butter, softened
½ teaspoon vanilla extract
⅔ cup (150g) caster sugar
2 eggs
1 cup (150g) dried mixed berries
½ cup (70g) slivered almonds
⅔ cup (100g) plain flour
⅓ cup (50g) self-raising flour
¼ cup (60ml) milk

Sugared fruit

150g fresh blueberries
120g fresh raspberries
1 egg white, beaten lightly
2 tablespoons vanilla sugar

Cream cheese frosting

30g butter, softened
80g cream cheese, softened
1½ cups (240g) icing sugar

1 Prepare sugared fruit.
2 Preheat oven to moderately slow (170°C/150°C fan-forced). Line 6-hole texas or 12-hole standard muffin pan with paper cases.
3 Beat butter, extract, sugar and eggs in small bowl with electric mixer until light and fluffy.
4 Stir in fruit and nuts, then sifted flours and milk. Divide mixture among cases; smooth surface.
5 Bake large cakes about 45 minutes, small cakes about 35 minutes. Turn cakes onto wire rack to cool.
6 Make cream cheese frosting.
7 Spread cakes with frosting. Decorate with sugared fruit.

Sugared fruit

Brush each berry lightly with egg white; roll fruit in sugar. Place fruit on baking paper-lined tray. Leave about 1 hour or until sugar is dry.

Cream cheese frosting

Beat butter and cheese in small bowl with electric mixer until light and fluffy; gradually beat in sifted icing sugar.

pear butterfly cakes

Pear and maple buttercake

1 medium fresh pear (230g),
    grated coarsely
60g butter, softened
¼ cup (35g) self-raising flour
¾ cup (110g) plain flour
1 teaspoon ground cinnamon
½ cup (110g) firmly packed
    brown sugar
¼ cup (60ml) maple-flavoured
    syrup
2 eggs
⅓ cup (40g) coarsely chopped
    pecans
⅓ cup (55g) finely chopped
    dried pear

Pear butterflies

1 tablespoon caster sugar
1 tablespoon water
1 medium brown pear (230g)
    (eg. beurre bosc), sliced thinly

Fondant icing

500g white prepared fondant,
    chopped coarsely
1 egg white
blue, pink and yellow food
    colouring

1 Make pear butterflies.
2 Preheat oven to moderate
(180°C/160°C fan-forced). Line
6-hole texas or 12-hole standard
muffin pan with paper cases.
3 Drain fresh pear, squeezing out
as much juice as possible. You
need ⅔ cup grated pear.
4 Beat butter, flours, cinnamon,
sugar, syrup and eggs in small
bowl with electric mixer on low
speed until ingredients are
combined. Beat on medium
speed until mixture is changed
to a paler colour.
5 Stir in fresh pear, nuts and dried
pear. Divide mixture among cases;
smooth surface.
6 Bake large cakes about
35 minutes, small cakes about
30 minutes. Turn cakes onto
wire rack to cool.
7 Make fondant icing. Divide
icing into three small bowls; using
colourings, tint icing pale blue,
pink and yellow. Spoon icing
quickly over cakes, level with tops
of cases; allow to set.
8 Top cakes with pear slices.

Pear butterflies

Preheat oven to very slow (120°C/
100°C fan-forced). Combine sugar
and the water in small saucepan.
Stir over medium heat, without
boiling, until sugar is dissolved.
Bring to a boil, reduce heat;
simmer, without stirring, 1 minute.
Brush pear slices both sides with
sugar syrup. Place slices in a
single layer on a wire rack over
oven tray (see page 115). Dry in
oven about 40 minutes. While
pears are still warm, shape into
butterfly wings (see page 115).
Cool on wire rack.

Fondant icing

Place fondant in a medium
bowl over a medium saucepan
of simmering water; stir until
smooth. Stir in egg white.
Stand at room temperature
for about 10 minutes or until
thickened slightly.

Chocolate ginger cake
½ cup (110g) firmly packed
   brown sugar
½ cup (75g) plain flour
½ cup (75g) self-raising flour
¼ teaspoon bicarbonate of soda
1 teaspoon ground ginger
½ teaspoon ground cinnamon
¼ teaspoon ground nutmeg
90g butter, softened
1 egg
¼ cup (60ml) buttermilk
2 tablespoons golden syrup
50g dark eating chocolate,
   chopped coarsely

Decorations
300ml thickened cream
3 x 50g violet crumble bars,
   chopped coarsely

1 Preheat oven to moderately slow (170°C/150°C fan-forced). Line 6-hole texas or 12-hole standard muffin pan with paper cases.
2 Sift dry ingredients into small bowl, add butter, egg, buttermilk and syrup; beat mixture with electric mixer on low speed until ingredients are combined. Increase speed to medium, beat until mixture is changed to a paler colour. Stir in chocolate. Divide mixture among cases; smooth surface.
3 Bake large cakes about 40 minutes, small cakes about 30 minutes. Turn cakes onto wire rack to cool.
4 Spread cakes with whipped cream; top with violet crumble.

honeycomb creams

Vanilla buttercake
90g butter, softened
½ teaspoon vanilla extract
½ cup (110g) caster sugar
2 eggs
1 cup (150g) self-raising flour
2 tablespoons milk

Butter cream frosting
125g butter, softened
1½ cups (240g) icing sugar
2 tablespoons milk
50g dark eating chocolate,
    chopped finely
1 tablespoon cocoa powder
pink food colouring

Decorations
ice cream waffle cones
strawberry slices
toasted flaked coconut
finely grated dark eating
    chocolate

1 Preheat oven to moderate (180°C/160°C fan-forced). Line 6-hole texas or 12-hole standard muffin pan with paper cases.
2 Beat butter, extract, sugar, eggs, flour and milk in small bowl with electric mixer on low speed until ingredients are just combined. Increase speed to medium, beat until mixture is changed to a paler colour.
3 Divide mixture among cases; smooth surface.
4 Bake large cakes about 25 minutes, small cakes about 20 minutes. Turn cakes onto wire rack to cool.
5 Make butter cream frosting.
6 Remove cases from cakes. Using a serrated knife, shape cakes into balls (see page 114) so they sit inside waffle cones.
7 Place cakes in cones, spread with frosting; decorate with strawberries, coconut and grated chocolate.

Butter cream frosting
Beat butter in small bowl with electric mixer until light and fluffy; beat in sifted icing sugar and milk, in two batches. Divide mixture among four small bowls. Add chopped chocolate to one and sifted cocoa to another. Using colouring, tint one pink and leave one plain.

ice-cream cone cakes

Cream cheese lemon cake

90g butter, softened
90g cream cheese, softened
2 teaspoons finely grated
    lemon rind
²⁄₃ cup (150g) caster sugar
2 eggs
¹⁄₃ cup (50g) self-raising flour
½ cup (75g) plain flour

Meringue cases

3 egg whites
¾ cup (165g) caster sugar
1 tablespoon cornflour
1 teaspoon white vinegar
½ teaspoon vanilla extract

Decorations

300ml thickened cream, whipped
125g strawberries, quartered
1 tablespoon passionfruit pulp
½ cup (75g) blueberries
1 medium banana (230g),
    sliced thickly

1 Make meringue cases.
2 Preheat oven to moderate
(180°C/160°C fan-forced). Line
6-hole texas or 12-hole standard
muffin pan with paper cases.
3 Beat butter, cheese, rind, sugar
and eggs in small bowl with
electric mixer until light and fluffy.
4 Add flours to cheese mixture;
beat on low speed until combined.
Divide mixture among cases;
smooth surface.
5 Bake large cakes about
30 minutes, small cakes about
20 minutes. Turn cakes onto
wire rack to cool.
6 Drop a teaspoon of whipped
cream on each cake; top with
meringue cases. Spoon remaining
cream into cases and decorate
with fruit.

Meringue cases

Preheat oven to very slow
(120°C/100°C fan-forced). Grease
oven tray; line base with baking
paper, trace six 8.5cm circles
onto paper for large cakes,
and 12 x 5.5cm circles for small
cakes. Beat egg whites in small
bowl with electric mixer until
soft peaks form. Gradually add
sugar, a tablespoon at a time,
beating until sugar dissolves
between additions. Fold in
cornflour, vinegar and extract.
Spoon meringue inside circles
on tray; hollow out slightly. Bake
45 minutes or until cases are firm.
Cool in oven with door ajar.

lemon pavlova puffs

choc-mint mousse cakes

Double chocolate mint cake

125g box (16) square after
   dinner mints
60g dark eating chocolate,
   chopped coarsely
⅔ cup (160ml) water
90g butter, softened
½ teaspoon peppermint essence
1 cup (220g) firmly packed
   brown sugar
2 eggs
⅔ cup (100g) self-raising flour
2 tablespoons cocoa powder
⅓ cup (40g) almond meal
1 tablespoon cocoa powder,
   extra

Chocolate mousse

150g dark eating chocolate,
   chopped roughly
½ teaspoon peppermint essence
¾ cup (180ml) thickened cream
2 eggs, separated
2 tablespoons caster sugar

1 Make chocolate mousse.
2 Preheat oven to moderately slow (170°C/150°C fan-forced). Line 6-hole texas or 12-hole standard muffin pan with paper cases.
3 For large cakes, using a 3.5cm long petal cutter, cut out 2 petals from each after dinner mint. For small cakes use a 1cm long petal cutter, to cut 4 petals from each after dinner mint. Coarsely chop off-cuts, reserve for cake mixture.
4 Combine chocolate and the water in small saucepan; stir over low heat until smooth.
5 Beat butter, essence, sugar and eggs in small bowl with electric mixer until light and fluffy.
6 Stir in sifted flour and cocoa, almond meal, warm chocolate mixture and reserved after dinner mints. Divide mixture among cases; smooth surface.
7 Bake large cakes about 40 minutes, small cakes about 30 minutes. Turn cakes onto wire rack to cool.
8 Place a lightly greased collar of foil around each cake. Divide firm chocolate mousse evenly among tops of cakes. Freeze cakes for about 30 minutes to help set the mousse quickly.

9 Dust mousse with extra sifted cocoa; arrange petals on top in a flower. Gently remove foil; dip spatula in hot water and smooth side of mousse.

Chocolate mousse

Combine chocolate, essence and half the cream in a medium heatproof bowl over a medium saucepan of simmering water; stir until smooth. Cool mixture 5 minutes, then stir in egg yolks. Beat remaining cream in small bowl with electric mixer until soft peaks form. Beat egg whites in another small bowl with electric mixer until soft peaks form; add sugar gradually, beat until dissolved. Fold cream into chocolate mixture, then egg whites. Spoon mixture into a shallow baking dish. Cover, refrigerate 4 hours or until firm.

sugar & lace

Caramel mud cake

125g butter, chopped coarsely
100g white eating chocolate,
    chopped coarsely
⅔ cup (150g) firmly packed
    brown sugar
¼ cup (90g) golden syrup
⅔ cup (160ml) milk
1 cup (150g) plain flour
⅓ cup (50g) self-raising flour
1 egg

Decorations

doily, lace or stencil
½ cup (80g) icing sugar

1 Preheat oven to moderately slow
(170°C/150°C fan-forced). Line
6-hole texas or 12-hole standard
muffin pan with paper cases.
2 Combine butter, chocolate,
sugar, syrup and milk in small
saucepan; stir over low heat,
until smooth. Transfer mixture to
medium bowl; cool 15 minutes.
3 Whisk sifted flours into
chocolate mixture, then egg.
Divide mixture among cases.
4 Bake large cakes about
40 minutes, small cakes about
30 minutes. Turn cakes onto
wire rack to cool.
5 Place doily, lace or stencil
over cake; sift a little icing sugar
over doily (see page 114), then
carefully lift doily from cake.
Repeat with remaining cakes
and icing sugar.

cloud cakes

Strawberry swirl buttercake

90g butter, softened
½ teaspoon vanilla extract
½ cup (110g) caster sugar
2 eggs
1 cup (150g) self-raising flour
2 tablespoons milk
2 tablespoons strawberry jam

Fluffy frosting

1 cup (220g) caster sugar
⅓ cup (80ml) water
2 egg whites

Decorations

pink coloured sugar
   (see page 115)

1 Preheat oven to moderate (180°C/160°C fan-forced). Line 6-hole texas or 12-hole standard muffin pan with paper cases.
2 Beat butter, extract, sugar, eggs, flour and milk in small bowl with electric mixer on low speed until ingredients are just combined. Increase speed to medium, beat until mixture is changed to a paler colour.
3 Divide mixture among cases; smooth surface. Divide jam over tops of cakes; using a skewer swirl jam into cakes.
4 Bake large cakes about 30 minutes, small cakes about 20 minutes. Turn cakes onto wire rack to cool.
5 Make fluffy frosting.
6 Spread cakes with fluffy frosting; sprinkle with coloured sugar.

Fluffy frosting
Combine sugar and the water in small saucepan; stir over heat, without boiling, until sugar is dissolved. Boil, uncovered, without stirring about 5 minutes or until syrup reaches 116°C on a candy thermometer. Syrup should be thick but not coloured. Remove from heat, allow bubbles to subside. Beat egg whites in small bowl with electric mixer until soft peaks form. While mixer is operating, add hot syrup in thin stream; beat on high speed about 10 minutes or until mixture is thick and cool.

toffee-apple towers

Maple, pecan and apple cake

60g butter, softened
1 cup (150g) self-raising flour
1 teaspoon ground cinnamon
½ cup (110g) firmly packed
    brown sugar
¼ cup (60ml) maple-flavoured
    syrup
2 eggs
⅔ cup (80g) coarsely chopped
    pecans
½ cup (85g) coarsely grated
    apple

Maple frosting

90g butter, softened
1 cup (160g) icing sugar
2 teaspoons maple-flavoured
    syrup

Toffee

1 cup (220g) caster sugar
½ cup (125ml) water

1 Preheat oven to moderate
(180°C/160°C fan-forced). Line
6-hole texas or 12-hole standard
muffin pan with paper cases.
2 Beat butter, flour, cinnamon,
sugar, syrup and eggs in small
bowl with electric mixer on low
speed until ingredients are
combined. Increase speed to
medium, beat until mixture is
changed to a paler colour.
3 Stir in nuts and grated apple.
Divide mixture among cases;
smooth surface.
4 Bake large cakes about
35 minutes, small cakes about
25 minutes. Turn cakes onto
wire rack to cool.
5 Make maple frosting.
Make toffee.
6 Spread cakes with frosting;
decorate with toffee shards.

Maple frosting

Beat butter, sifted icing sugar and
syrup in small bowl with electric
mixer until light and fluffy.

Toffee

Combine sugar with the water in
small heavy-based saucepan. Stir
over heat, without boiling, until
sugar dissolves; bring to the boil.
Reduce heat; simmer, uncovered,
without stirring, until mixture is
golden brown. Remove from heat;
stand until bubbles subside. Make
toffee shards on baking paper-
lined oven tray (see page 109).

turkish delights

White chocolate pistachio cake

60g white eating chocolate, chopped roughly
2 tablespoons rose water
½ cup (125ml) water
⅓ cup (45g) pistachio nuts
90g butter, softened
1 cup (220g) firmly packed brown sugar
2 eggs
⅔ cup (100g) self-raising flour
2 tablespoons plain flour

Decorations

⅔ cup (90g) coarsely chopped pistachio nuts
300g white eating chocolate, melted
900g turkish delight, chopped

1 Preheat oven to moderate (180°C/160°C fan-forced). Line 6-hole texas or 12-hole standard muffin pan with paper cases.
2 Combine chocolate, rose water and the water in small saucepan; stir over low heat until smooth.
3 Blend or process nuts until fine.
4 Beat butter, sugar and eggs in small bowl with electric mixer until combined.
5 Fold in sifted flours, ground pistachios and warm chocolate mixture. Divide among cases.
6 Bake large cakes about 35 minutes, small cakes about 25 minutes. Turn cakes onto wire rack to cool.
7 Cut a 3cm deep hole in the centre of each cake; fill with a few chopped nuts. Drizzle with a little chocolate; replace lids.
8 Decorate cakes with pieces of turkish delight and chopped nuts dipped in chocolate.

rocky road cakes

Marble cake

125g butter, softened
½ teaspoon vanilla extract
⅔ cup (150g) caster sugar
2 eggs
1¼ cups (185g) self-raising flour
⅓ cup (80ml) milk
pink food colouring
1 tablespoon cocoa powder
2 teaspoons milk, extra

Rocky road topping

½ cup (70g) unsalted roasted
   peanuts
1 cup (200g) red glacé cherries,
   halved
1 cup (100g) pink and white
   marshmallows, chopped
   coarsely
½ cup (25g) flaked coconut,
   toasted
200g milk eating chocolate,
   melted

Decorations

50g milk chocolate Melts,
   melted

1 Preheat oven to moderate (180°C/160°C fan-forced). Line 6-hole texas or 12-hole standard muffin pan with paper cases.
2 Beat butter, extract, sugar and eggs in small bowl with electric mixer until light and fluffy. Stir in sifted flour and milk in two batches.
3 Divide mixture evenly among three bowls. Tint one mixture pink. Blend sifted cocoa with extra milk in cup; stir into another mixture. Leave third mixture plain.
4 Drop alternate spoonfuls of the mixtures into cases. Pull a skewer backwards and forwards through mixtures for a marbled effect; smooth surface.
5 Bake large cakes about 30 minutes, small cakes about 20 minutes. Turn cakes onto wire rack to cool.
6 Combine ingredients for rocky road topping in medium bowl.
7 Place topping on tops of cakes; drizzle with chocolate.

lamington angels

Vanilla buttercake

90g butter, softened
½ teaspoon vanilla extract
½ cup (110g) caster sugar
2 eggs
1 cup (150g) self-raising flour
2 tablespoons milk

Chocolate icing

10g butter
⅓ cup (80ml) milk
2 cups (320g) icing sugar
¼ cup (25g) cocoa powder

Decorations

1 cup (80g) desiccated coconut
¼ cup (100g) raspberry jam
½ cup (125ml) thickened cream,
    whipped

1 Preheat oven to moderate (180°C/160°C fan-forced). Line 6-hole texas or 12-hole standard muffin pan with paper cases.
2 Beat butter, extract, sugar, eggs, flour and milk in small bowl with electric mixer on low speed until ingredients are just combined. Increase speed to medium, beat until mixture is changed to a paler colour.
3 Divide mixture among cases; smooth surface.
4 Bake large cakes about 25 minutes, small cakes about 20 minutes. Turn cakes onto wire rack to cool.
5 Make chocolate icing.
6 Remove cases from cakes. Dip cakes in icing; drain off excess, toss cakes in coconut. Place cakes on wire rack to set.
7 Cut cakes as desired; fill with jam and cream.

Chocolate icing

Melt butter in medium heatproof bowl over medium saucepan of simmering water. Stir in milk and sifted icing sugar and cocoa until icing is a coating consistency.

Ginger buttermilk cake

½ cup (110g) firmly packed
   brown sugar
½ cup (75g) plain flour
½ cup (75g) self-raising flour
¼ teaspoon bicarbonate of soda
1 teaspoon ground ginger
½ teaspoon ground cinnamon
¼ teaspoon ground nutmeg
90g butter, softened
1 egg
¼ cup (60ml) buttermilk
2 tablespoons golden syrup

Decorations

½ cup (80g) icing sugar
400g white prepared fondant
⅓ cup (110g) ginger marmalade,
   warmed, strained
50g red prepared fondant
50g black prepared fondant

1 Preheat oven to moderately slow (170°C/150°C fan-forced). Line 6-hole texas or 12-hole standard muffin pan with paper cases.
2 Sift dry ingredients into small bowl, then add remaining ingredients. Beat mixture with electric mixer on low speed until ingredients are combined. Increase speed to medium, beat until mixture is changed to a paler colour.
3 Divide mixture among cases; smooth surface.
4 Bake large cakes about 40 minutes, small cakes about 30 minutes. Turn cakes onto wire rack to cool.
5 Dust surface with sifted icing sugar; knead white prepared fondant until smooth. Roll out fondant to a thickness of 5mm. Cut out rounds large enough to cover tops of cakes.

6 Brush tops of cakes with marmalade; cover with fondant rounds (see page 110).
7 Roll out red and black fondants, separately, until 5mm thick. Cut out shapes using heart, diamond, club and spade cutters (see page 105).
8 Roll out red and black fondant scraps, separately, to a thickness of 2mm. Cut out 'A's using an alphabet cutter set (see page 105).
9 Secure fondant shapes to cakes by brushing backs with a tiny amount of water.

sweet ginger aces

coconut kisses

White chocolate mud cake

125g butter, chopped coarsely
80g white eating chocolate,
    chopped coarsely
1 cup (220g) caster sugar
½ cup (125ml) milk
½ cup (75g) plain flour
½ cup (75g) self-raising flour
½ teaspoon coconut essence
1 egg

Whipped white chocolate ganache

¼ cup (60ml) cream
185g white eating chocolate,
    chopped coarsely
1 tablespoon coconut liqueur

Decorations

3 x 150g boxes ferrero raffaelo
    chocolate truffles

1 Preheat oven to moderately slow (170°C/150°C fan-forced). Line 6-hole texas or 12-hole standard muffin pan with paper cases.
2 Combine butter, chocolate, sugar and milk in small saucepan; stir over low heat until smooth. Transfer mixture to medium bowl; cool 15 minutes.
3 Whisk in sifted flours, then essence and egg. Divide mixture among cases; smooth surface.
4 Bake large cakes about 40 minutes, small cakes about 30 minutes. Turn cakes onto wire rack to cool.
5 Make whipped white chocolate ganache.
6 Spread cakes with ganache. Top with halved truffles, then stack with whole truffles using a little ganache to secure.

Whipped white chocolate ganache

Bring cream to a boil in small saucepan; pour over chocolate and liqueur in small bowl of electric mixer, stir until smooth. Cover; refrigerate 30 minutes. Beat with an electric mixer until light and fluffy.

froufrou

Raspberry coconut cake

125g butter, softened
1 cup (220g) caster sugar
3 eggs
½ cup (75g) plain flour
¼ cup (35g) self-raising flour
½ cup (40g) desiccated coconut
⅓ cup (80g) sour cream
150g frozen raspberries

Cream cheese frosting

60g butter, softened
160g cream cheese, softened
2 teaspoons coconut essence
3 cups (480g) icing sugar

Decorations

1 cup (50g) flaked coconut, toasted
15 fresh raspberries, halved

1 Preheat oven to moderate (180°C/160°C fan-forced). Line 6-hole texas or 12-hole standard muffin pan with paper cases.
2 Beat butter, sugar and eggs in small bowl with electric mixer until light and fluffy.
3 Stir in sifted flours, coconut, cream and frozen raspberries. Divide mixture among cases; smooth surface.
4 Bake large cakes about 50 minutes, small cakes about 40 minutes. Turn cakes onto wire rack to cool.
5 Make cream cheese frosting.
6 Remove cases from cakes; spread cakes with frosting.
7 Decorate cakes with coconut and raspberries.

Cream cheese frosting

Beat butter, cream cheese and essence in small bowl with electric mixer until light and fluffy; gradually beat in sifted icing sugar.

SARTRE   L'être et le néant

WITTGENSTEIN   Tractatus logico-philosophicus

JEAN
ECHENOZ   LE
MÉRIDIEN
DE
GREENWICH   ☆M

mochaccinos

You will need six 350ml or twelve 125ml capacity coffee cups for this recipe.

Mocha mud cake

165g butter, chopped coarsely
100g dark eating chocolate, chopped coarsely
1⅓ cups (290g) caster sugar
⅔ cup (170ml) water
¼ cup (60ml) coffee liqueur
2 tablespoons instant coffee granules
1 cup (150g) plain flour
2 tablespoons self-raising flour
2 tablespoons cocoa powder
1 egg

Decorations

300ml carton thickened cream, whipped
2 tablespoons chocolate-flavoured topping
1 tablespoon cocoa powder

1 Preheat oven to moderately slow (170°C/150°C fan-forced). Line 6-hole texas or 12-hole standard muffin pan with paper cases.
2 Combine butter, chocolate, sugar, the water, liqueur and coffee in small saucepan; stir over low heat until smooth.
3 Transfer mixture to medium bowl; cool 15 minutes. Whisk in sifted flours and cocoa, then egg. Divide mixture among cases.
4 Bake large cakes about 1 hour, small cakes about 50 minutes. Turn cakes onto wire rack to cool.
5 Remove cases from cakes. Place cakes in coffee cups, top with cream. Place chocolate topping into piping bag fitted with small plain tube, pipe spirals over cream; feather and fan cakes by pulling a skewer through the spirals (see page 114) or, dust cakes with sifted cocoa.

florentine cakes

Double chocolate mud cake
60g dark eating chocolate, chopped coarsely
⅔ cup (160ml) water
90g butter, softened
1 cup (220g) firmly packed brown sugar
2 eggs
⅔ cup (100g) self-raising flour
2 tablespoons cocoa powder
⅓ cup (40g) almond meal

Milk chocolate ganache
100g milk eating chocolate, chopped coarsely
¼ cup (60ml) cream

Florentine topping
1 cup (80g) flaked almonds, toasted
½ cup (115g) coarsely chopped glacé ginger
1 cup (200g) red glacé cherries, halved

Decorations
50g dark eating chocolate, melted

1 Preheat oven to moderately slow (170°C/150°C fan-forced). Line 6-hole texas or 12-hole standard muffin pan with paper cases.
2 Combine chocolate and the water in small saucepan; stir over low heat until smooth.
3 Beat butter, sugar and eggs in small bowl with electric mixer until light and fluffy.
4 Stir in sifted flour and cocoa, almond meal and warm chocolate mixture. Divide mixture among cases; smooth surface.
5 Bake large cakes about 35 minutes, small cakes about 25 minutes. Turn cakes onto wire rack to cool.
6 Make milk chocolate ganache.
7 Combine ingredients for florentine topping in small bowl.
8 Spread cakes with ganache, top with florentine mixture; drizzle with chocolate.

Milk chocolate ganache
Bring cream to a boil in small saucepan, pour over chocolate in small bowl; stir until smooth. Stand at room temperature until ganache is spreadable.

baby blue

60g dark eating chocolate,
  chopped coarsely
1 teaspoon finely grated
  orange rind
⅔ cup (160ml) orange juice
90g butter, softened
1 cup (220g) firmly packed
  brown sugar
2 eggs
⅔ cup (100g) self-raising flour
2 tablespoons cocoa powder
⅓ cup (40g) almond meal

Decorations
½ cup (80g) icing sugar
400g white prepared fondant
blue food colouring
⅓ cup (110g) orange marmalade,
  warmed, strained
2m ribbon, approximately

1 Preheat oven to moderately slow (170°C/150°C fan-forced). Line 6-hole texas or 12-hole standard muffin pan with paper cases.
2 Combine chocolate, rind and juice in small saucepan; stir over low heat until smooth.
3 Beat butter, sugar and eggs in small bowl with electric mixer until light and fluffy.
4 Stir in sifted flour and cocoa, almond meal and warm chocolate mixture. Divide mixture among cases; smooth surface.
5 Bake large cakes about 35 minutes, small cakes about 25 minutes. Turn cakes onto wire rack to cool.
6 Dust surface with sifted icing sugar, knead fondant until smooth. Knead blue colouring into fondant (see page 110).
7 Brush tops of cakes with marmalade. Roll fondant out to 5mm thickness; cut rounds large enough to cover tops of cakes.
8 Place rounds on cakes; tie cakes with ribbon.

tiramisu

Vanilla buttercake
90g butter, softened
½ teaspoon vanilla extract
½ cup (110g) caster sugar
2 eggs
1 cup (150g) self-raising flour
2 tablespoons milk

Mascarpone cream
250g mascarpone cheese
¼ cup (40g) icing sugar
1 tablespoon marsala
¾ cup (180ml) thickened cream,
   whipped

Coffee mixture
1 tablespoon instant coffee
   granules
⅓ cup (80ml) boiling water
2 tablespoons marsala

Decorations
50g dark eating chocolate,
   grated finely

1 Preheat oven to moderate (180°C/160°C fan-forced). Line 6-hole texas or 12-hole standard muffin pan with paper cases.
2 Beat butter, extract, sugar, eggs, flour and milk in small bowl with electric mixer on low speed until ingredients are just combined. Increase speed to medium, beat until mixture is changed to a paler colour. Divide mixture among cases; smooth surface.
3 Bake large cakes about 25 minutes, small cakes about 20 minutes. Turn cakes onto wire rack to cool.
4 Make mascarpone cream. Make coffee mixture.
5 Remove cases from cakes. Cut each cake horizontally into four. Brush both sides of cake slices with coffee mixture. Join cake slices with mascarpone cream.
6 Spread tops of cakes with mascarpone cream; sprinkle with grated chocolate. Refrigerate for 3 hours before serving.

Mascarpone cream
Combine mascarpone, sifted icing sugar and marsala in small bowl; fold in cream.

Coffee mixture
Combine coffee, the water and marsala in small bowl; cool.

lemon cheesecakes

Lemon cheesecake

100g plain sweet biscuits

50g butter, melted

2 x 250g packets cream cheese, softened

2 teaspoons finely grated lemon rind

½ cup (110g) caster sugar

2 eggs

Glaze

⅔ cup (220g) apricot jam

2 tablespoons brandy

1 Preheat oven to slow (150°C/130°C fan-forced). Line 6-hole texas or 12-hole standard muffin pan with paper cases.

2 Blend or process biscuits until fine. Add butter; process until just combined. Divide mixture among cases; press firmly. Refrigerate 30 minutes.

3 Beat cheese, rind and sugar in small bowl with electric mixer until smooth. Beat in eggs. Pour mixture into cases.

4 Bake large cakes about 30 minutes, small cakes about 25 minutes. Cool.

5 Make glaze.

6 Pour glaze evenly over tops of cheesecakes; refrigerate 2 hours or until glaze is set.

Glaze

Heat jam and brandy in small saucepan over low heat; strain.

Fig, caramel and walnut cake

125g butter, softened
½ teaspoon vanilla extract
⅔ cup (150g) caster sugar
2 eggs
¾ cup (150g) finely chopped
   dried figs
½ cup (60g) finely chopped
   walnuts
⅔ cup (100g) plain flour
⅓ cup (50g) self-raising flour
60g mars bar, chopped finely
¼ cup (60ml) milk

Whipped milk chocolate ganache

⅓ cup (80ml) cream
200g milk eating chocolate

Toffee

½ cup (110g) caster sugar
¼ cup (60ml) water

Decorations

6 medium fresh figs (360g),
   quartered

1 Preheat oven to moderate (180°C/160°C fan-forced). Line 6-hole texas or 12-hole standard muffin pan with paper cases.
2 Beat butter, extract, sugar and eggs in small bowl with electric mixer until light and fluffy.
3 Stir in figs, nuts, sifted flours, mars bar and milk. Divide mixture among cases; smooth surface.
4 Bake large cakes about 40 minutes, small cakes about 30 minutes. Turn cakes onto wire rack to cool.
5 Make whipped milk chocolate ganache.
6 Make toffee; form into shapes over rolling pin (see page 109).
7 Spread cakes with ganache; decorate with fig quarters and toffee shapes.

Whipped milk chocolate ganache

Bring cream to a boil in small saucepan, pour over chocolate in small bowl of electric mixer, stir until smooth. Cover, refrigerate for 30 minutes. Beat with electric mixer until light and fluffy.

Toffee

Combine sugar with the water in small heavy-based saucepan. Stir over heat, without boiling, until sugar dissolves; bring to the boil. Reduce heat; simmer, uncovered, without stirring, until mixture is golden brown. Remove from heat; stand until bubbles subside.

fig and toffee crowns

orange blossom cakes

Orange, almond and
craisin cake

125g butter, softened
2 teaspoons finely grated
   orange rind
⅔ cup (150g) caster sugar
2 eggs
1 cup (150g) self-raising flour
⅓ cup (50g) plain flour
⅓ cup (40g) almond meal
½ cup (65g) craisins
¼ cup (60ml) orange juice
2 tablespoons milk

Modelling fondant

2 teaspoons gelatine
1½ tablespoons water
2 teaspoons glucose syrup
1½ cups (240g) pure icing sugar
½ cup (80g) pure icing sugar,
   extra
yellow, orange and pink food
   colouring

Butter cream

90g butter, softened
¼ teaspoon orange essence
1 cup (160g) icing sugar
1 tablespoon milk
yellow, orange and pink food
   colouring

1 Make modelling fondant;
reserve a walnut-sized portion.
2 Dust surface with pure icing
sugar, roll remaining fondant to a
thickness of approximately 3mm.
Cut out 18 flowers using 3cm
cutter or 36 flowers using 2cm
cutter (see page 105).
3 Divide reserved fondant into
three; knead one of the colourings
into each portion. Roll tiny balls
for flower centres; lightly brush
flower centres with water to secure
coloured balls.
4 Preheat oven to moderate
(180°C/160°C fan-forced). Line
6-hole texas or 12-hole standard
muffin pan with paper cases.
5 Beat butter, rind, sugar and
eggs in small bowl with electric
mixer until light and fluffy.
6 Stir in sifted flours, almond
meal, craisins, juice and milk.
Divide mixture among cases;
smooth surface.
7 Bake large cakes about
35 minutes, small cakes about
25 minutes. Turn cakes onto
wire rack to cool.
8 Make butter cream.
9 Spread cakes with butter cream;
decorate with flowers.

Modelling fondant

Sprinkle gelatine over the water in
cup; stand cup in small saucepan
of simmering water, stirring
until gelatine is dissolved, add
glucose. Place half the sifted
icing sugar in small bowl, stir in
gelatine mixture. Gradually stir
in remaining sifted icing sugar,
knead on surface dusted with
extra sifted icing sugar until
smooth. Enclose in plastic wrap.

Butter cream

Beat butter and essence in small
bowl with electric mixer until light
and fluffy. Beat in sifted icing sugar
and milk, in two batches. Beat in a
little of desired colouring.

neapolitan cakes

Marbled buttercake
125g butter, softened
½ teaspoon vanilla extract
⅔ cup (150g) caster sugar
2 eggs
1¼ cups (185g) self-raising flour
⅓ cup (80ml) milk
pink food colouring
1 tablespoon cocoa powder
2 teaspoons milk, extra

Butter cream
125g butter, softened
1½ cups (240g) icing sugar
2 tablespoons milk
pink food colouring
1 tablespoon cocoa powder
2 teaspoons milk, extra

1 Preheat oven to moderate (180°C/160°C fan-forced). Line 6-hole texas or 12-hole standard muffin pan with paper cases.
2 Beat butter, extract, sugar and eggs in small bowl with electric mixer until light and fluffy. Stir in sifted flour and milk, in two batches.
3 Divide mixture evenly among three bowls. Tint one mixture pink. Blend sifted cocoa with extra milk in cup; stir into another mixture. Leave third mixture plain.
4 Drop alternate spoonfuls of the three mixtures into cases. Pull a skewer backwards and forwards through mixtures for a marbled effect; smooth surface.
5 Bake large cakes about 30 minutes, small cakes about 20 minutes. Turn cakes onto wire rack to cool.
6 Make butter cream.
7 Spread cakes with the three colours of butter cream.

Butter cream
Beat butter in small bowl with electric mixer until as white as possible; beat in sifted icing sugar and milk, in two batches. Divide mixture evenly among three bowls. Tint one mixture pink. Blend sifted cocoa with extra milk in cup; stir into another mixture. Leave third mixture plain.

kaleidocakes

Orange buttercake
90g butter, softened
90g cream cheese, softened
2 teaspoons finely grated
    orange rind
⅔ cup (150g) caster sugar
2 eggs
⅓ cup (50g) self-raising flour
½ cup (75g) plain flour

Fondant icing
300g white prepared fondant,
    chopped coarsely
1 egg white
¼ teaspoon orange essence

Royal icing
1½ cups (240g) pure icing sugar
1 egg white
½ teaspoon lemon juice
yellow, orange, green, pink and
    purple food colouring

1 Preheat oven to moderate (180°C/160°C fan-forced). Line 6-hole texas or 12-hole standard muffin pan with paper cases.
2 Beat butter, cheese, rind, sugar and eggs in small bowl with electric mixer until light and fluffy.
3 Beat in flours on low speed until just combined. Divide mixture among cases; smooth surface.
4 Bake large cakes about 30 minutes, small cakes about 20 minutes. Turn cakes onto wire rack to cool.
5 Make fondant icing. Spread over cakes; allow to set at room temperature.
6 Make royal icing. Divide evenly among five small bowls. Using colourings, tint icing yellow, orange, green, pink and purple; cover each tightly with plastic wrap. Pipe patterns (see page 112) using picture as a guide.

Fondant icing
Place icing in a small bowl over a small saucepan of simmering water; stir until smooth. Stir in egg white and essence. Stand at room temperature for 10 minutes or until thickened slightly. Spread fondant quickly over cakes; use a metal spatula dipped in hot water to smooth surface.

Royal icing
Sift icing sugar through very fine sieve. Lightly beat egg white in small bowl with electric mixer; add icing sugar, a tablespoon at a time. When icing reaches firm peaks, use a wooden spoon to beat in juice; cover tightly with plastic wrap.

banana caramel cakes

Sour cream banana cake

90g butter, softened
½ cup (110g) firmly packed
   brown sugar
2 eggs
½ cup (75g) self-raising flour
½ cup (75g) plain flour
½ teaspoon bicarbonate
   of soda
½ teaspoon mixed spice
⅔ cup mashed overripe banana
⅓ cup (80g) sour cream
2 tablespoons milk

Filling and decorations

380g can top 'n' fill caramel
½ cup (125ml) thickened cream,
   whipped
2 medium bananas (400g),
   sliced thinly
100g dark eating chocolate

1 Preheat oven to moderate (180°C/160°C fan-forced). Line 6-hole texas or 12-hole standard muffin pan with paper cases.
2 Beat butter, sugar and eggs in small bowl with electric mixer until light and fluffy.
3 Stir in sifted dry ingredients, banana, sour cream and milk. Divide mixture among cases; smooth surface.
4 Bake large cakes about 25 minutes, small cakes about 20 minutes. Turn cakes onto wire rack to cool.
5 Remove cases from cakes.
6 Fold 2 tablespoons of the caramel into cream.
7 Cut cakes horizontally into three slices. Re-assemble cakes with remaining caramel and banana. Top with caramel-flavoured cream.
8 Using a vegetable peeler, grate chocolate (see page 106); sprinkle over cakes.

lemon meringue cakes

Coconut lemon curd cake

125g butter, softened
2 teaspoons finely grated
  lemon rind
⅔ cup (150g) caster sugar
2 eggs
⅓ cup (80ml) milk
¾ cup (60g) desiccated coconut
1¼ cups (185g) self-raising flour

Lemon curd

4 egg yolks
⅓ cup (75g) caster sugar
2 teaspoons finely grated
  lemon rind
¼ cup (60ml) lemon juice
40g butter

Coconut meringue

4 egg whites
1 cup (220g) caster sugar
1⅓ cups (95g) shredded coconut,
  chopped finely

1 Make lemon curd.
2 Preheat oven to moderate
(180°C/160°C fan-forced). Line
6-hole texas or 12-hole standard
muffin pan with paper cases.
3 Beat butter, rind, sugar and
eggs in small bowl with electric
mixer until light and fluffy.
4 Stir in milk and coconut, then
sifted flour. Divide mixture
among cases; smooth surface.
5 Bake large cakes about
25 minutes, small cakes about
20 minutes. Turn cakes onto
wire rack to cool. Increase oven
to hot (220°C/200°C fan-forced).
6 Cut a 2cm deep hole in the
centre of each cake, fill with curd;
discard cake tops.
7 Make coconut meringue; spoon
into a piping bag fitted with a 1cm
plain tube.
8 Pipe meringue on top of each
cake (see page 112); place cakes
on oven tray.
9 Bake in hot oven 5 minutes or
until meringue is browned lightly.

Lemon curd

Combine ingredients in a small
heatproof bowl over small
saucepan of simmering water,
stirring constantly, until mixture
thickens slightly and coats the
back of a spoon. Remove from
heat. Cover tightly; refrigerate
curd until cold.

Coconut meringue

Beat egg whites in small bowl with
electric mixer until soft peaks form;
gradually add sugar, beating until
sugar dissolves. Fold in coconut.

sweetheart

Raspberry swirl cake

125g butter, softened
½ teaspoon vanilla extract
⅔ cup (150g) caster sugar
2 eggs
1¼ cups (185g) self-raising flour
⅓ cup (80ml) milk
pink food colouring
2 tablespoons raspberry jam

Decorations

½ cup (80g) icing sugar
350g white prepared fondant
⅓ cup (110g) raspberry jam,
    warmed, strained
¼ teaspoon vodka
¼ teaspoon pink petal dust

1 Preheat oven to moderate (180°C/160°C fan-forced). Line 6-hole texas or 12-hole standard muffin pan with paper cases.
2 Beat butter, extract, sugar and eggs in small bowl with electric mixer until light and fluffy. Stir in sifted flour and milk, in two batches.
3 Divide mixture evenly between two bowls. Tint one mixture pink; leave other mixture plain. Drop alternate spoonfuls of the two mixtures into cases.
4 Divide jam among cakes, pull a skewer backwards and forwards through mixtures for a swirling effect; smooth surface.
5 Bake large cakes about 30 minutes, small cakes about 20 minutes. Turn cakes onto wire rack to cool.
6 On surface dusted with sifted icing sugar, knead fondant until smooth. Tint fondant with pink colouring; knead into fondant only until marbled (see page 110). Roll out fondant to a thickness of 5mm. Cut out rounds large enough to cover tops of cakes.
7 Blend vodka with petal dust. Using a fine paint brush, paint mixture onto a heart-shaped rubber stamp; press lightly onto fondant rounds. Pinch edges of rounds with fingers.
8 Brush tops of cakes with jam; top with stamped rounds.

chocolate valentines

Double chocolate raspberry cake

60g dark eating chocolate, chopped coarsely
½ cup (125ml) water
90g butter, softened
1 cup (220g) firmly packed brown sugar
2 eggs
⅔ cup (100g) self-raising flour
2 tablespoons cocoa powder
⅓ cup (40g) almond meal
100g frozen raspberries

Decorations

2 tablespoons cocoa powder
900g chocolate prepared fondant
⅓ cup (110g) raspberry jam, warmed, strained
½ cup (80g) icing sugar
150g red prepared fondant
150g white prepared fondant
pink food colouring

1 Preheat oven to moderately slow (170°C/150°C fan-forced). Line 6-hole texas or 12-hole standard muffin pan with paper cases.
2 Combine chocolate and the water in small saucepan; stir over low heat until smooth.
3 Beat butter, sugar and eggs in small bowl with electric mixer until just combined.
4 Stir in sifted flour and cocoa, almond meal, then warm chocolate mixture; fold in raspberries. Divide among cases; smooth surface.
5 Bake large cakes about 55 minutes, small cakes about 45 minutes. Turn cakes onto wire rack to cool.
6 Remove cases from cakes. On a surface dusted with sifted cocoa, knead chocolate fondant until smooth. Roll out to a thickness of 5mm. Cut out rounds large enough to cover tops of cakes.

7 Brush cakes with jam; cover cakes with chocolate fondant.
8 On a surface dusted with sifted icing sugar, knead white and red fondant separately until smooth. Use colouring to tint 100g of the white fondant pink and remaining white fondant a paler pink.
9 Roll each coloured fondant to a thickness of 5mm. Using heart-shaped cutters of varying sizes (see page 105) to suit size of cakes, cut out hearts from fondants using picture as a guide.
10 Decorate cakes with fondant hearts, each brushed with a little water to secure to each other.

coconut cherry hearts

Choc-chip cherry cake
125g butter, softened
½ teaspoon coconut essence
⅔ cup (150g) caster sugar
2 eggs
⅓ cup (80ml) milk
½ cup (40g) desiccated coconut
⅓ cup (70g) red glacé cherries,
    chopped coarsely
50g dark eating chocolate,
    chopped coarsely
1 cup (150g) self-raising flour
¼ cup (35g) plain flour

Milk chocolate ganache
¼ cup (60ml) cream
100g milk eating chocolate,
    chopped coarsely

Decorations
150g white chocolate Melts,
    melted
pink food colouring

1 Preheat oven to moderate (180°C/160°C fan-forced). Line 6-hole texas or 12-hole standard muffin pan with paper cases.
2 Beat butter, essence, sugar and eggs in small bowl with electric mixer until combined.
3 Stir in milk, coconut, cherries and chocolate, then sifted flours. Divide mixture among cases; smooth surface.
4 Bake large cakes about 35 minutes, small cakes about 25 minutes. Turn cakes onto wire rack to cool.
5 Make milk chocolate ganache.
6 Divide white chocolate evenly among three small bowls; tint two portions with two different shades of pink (see page 107).
7 Make three paper piping bags (see page 107); spoon a different coloured chocolate mixture into each bag. Pipe different coloured heart shapes in varying sizes (see page 107), onto baking paper-lined oven tray. Set at room temperature.
8 Spread cakes with ganache; decorate with coloured hearts.

Milk chocolate ganache
Bring cream to a boil in small saucepan; pour over chocolate in small bowl, stir until smooth. Cover bowl; stand at room temperature until ganache is spreadable.

the wedding story

It's important to measure the cake mixture carefully, so the cakes are all the same depth. Make the full amount of mixture; it will be fine standing at room temperature while you bake the 70 cakes in batches. We used standard sized foil cases. You need 64 cakes for the story board. We used scrap booking decorations, available from craft and haberdashery shops and some newsagents.

White chocolate mud cake

500g butter, chopped coarsely
360g white eating chocolate, chopped coarsely
4 cups (880g) caster sugar
2 cups (500ml) milk
3 cups (450g) plain flour
1 cup (150g) self-raising flour
2 teaspoons vanilla extract
4 eggs

Fluffy mock cream frosting

2 tablespoons milk
⅓ cup (80ml) water
1 cup (220g) caster sugar
1 teaspoon gelatine
2 tablespoons water, extra
250g butter, softened
1 teaspoon vanilla extract

Royal icing

1½ cups (240g) pure icing sugar
1 egg white
½ teaspoon lemon juice

Decorations

60cm square cake board
wedding-themed decorations
3m silver ribbon

1 Preheat oven to moderately slow (170°C/150°C fan-forced). Line two 12-hole standard muffin pans with paper cases.
2 Stir butter, chocolate, sugar and milk in large saucepan, over low heat, until smooth. Transfer to large bowl; cool 15 minutes.
3 Whisk in sifted flours then extract and eggs. Drop exactly 2 level tablespoons of mixture into each case.
4 Bake cakes about 25 minutes. Turn onto wire rack to cool.
5 Meanwhile make fluffy mock cream frosting. Cover backs of decorations with baking paper to prevent them from absorbing the frosting.
6 Spread 64 cakes with frosting, place on cake board. Secure ribbon around cakes.
7 Make royal icing; spoon icing into a piping bag fitted with a small plain tube. Pipe hearts onto about 10 of the cakes.
8 Top remaining cakes with wedding-themed decorations.

Fluffy mock cream frosting

Combine milk, the water and sugar in small saucepan, stir over low heat, without boiling, until sugar is dissolved. Sprinkle gelatine over extra water in cup, add to pan; stir syrup until gelatine is dissolved. Cool to room temperature. Beat butter and extract in small bowl with electric mixer, until as white as possible. While motor is operating, gradually pour in cold syrup; beat until light and fluffy. Mixture will thicken on standing.

Royal icing

Sift icing sugar through very fine sieve. Lightly beat egg white in small bowl with electric mixer; add icing sugar, a tablespoon at a time. When icing reaches firm peaks, use a wooden spoon to beat in juice; cover tightly with plastic wrap.

wedding gift cakes

This cake is simply a stack of boxes each containing a cupcake for your wedding guests to take home. The choice of boxes, colours of ribbon and flowers is up to you. Choose the boxes first – size, colour, and quantity. For the ribbon, measure each box, allowing enough ribbon to wrap around and overlap slightly. Our cake has been assembled directly onto a table, but you could also use a covered board. Choose flowers that complement the rest of the wedding flowers. We topped the boxes with a traditional cake for the bride and groom to cut. Alternatively, use a stunning arrangement of flowers. The first recipe explains what we did, using 54 cupcakes. This is only a guide – make the stack larger or smaller, or have more take-home boxes set aside. Most cupcake recipes in this book make 6 texas or 12 standard muffin-sized cakes, you will have to work out the size, type and flavour of cake you'd like, and then work out how many batches of the recipe you'd need.

54 cupcakes
9cm square cake
10cm square cake board
400g white prepared fondant
¼ cup (100g) apricot jam, warmed, strained
400g prepared almond paste
½ cup (80g) icing sugar
20m ribbon
54 x 8cm square gift boxes

1 Bake cupcakes for gift boxes and 9cm square cake of your choice.
2 Secure square cake to board with small piece of fondant made into a paste with water. Brush cake all over with jam.
3 Knead almond paste on surface dusted with sifted icing sugar, cover cake (see page 110); stand overnight.
4 Brush almond paste with jam, cover cake with fondant (see page 110); stand overnight.
5 Secure ribbon to each box with glue or sticky tape.
6 Place one cupcake in each box; stack boxes. Position square cake on top. Decorate with flowers.

These recipes are for the cake on the top tier; use your favourite. All cakes are baked in a greased and lined deep 9cm square pan. A filigree textured plate was used to mark the fondant.

rich fruit cake
60g butter, softened
⅓ cup (75g) firmly packed brown sugar
1 egg
2 teaspoons orange marmalade
375g (2⅓ cups) mixed dried fruit, chopped finely
⅓ (50g) cup plain flour
¼ cup (35g) self-raising flour
½ teaspoon mixed spice
2 tablespoons sweet sherry
2 tablespoons sweet sherry, extra

1 Preheat oven to slow (150°C/130°C fan-forced).
2 Follow method for Christmas snowflakes on page 101 for cake.
3 Bake cake about 2 hours.

white chocolate mud cake
60g butter, chopped coarsely
40g white chocolate, chopped coarsely
½ cup (110g) caster sugar
¼ cup (60ml) milk
⅓ cup (50g) plain flour
2 tablespoons self-raising flour
½ teaspoon vanilla extract
1 egg, beaten lightly

1 Preheat oven to moderately slow (170°C/150°C fan-forced).
2 Follow method for Coconut kisses on page 31 for this cake.
3 Bake cake about 1 hour.

dark chocolate mud cake
80g butter, chopped coarsely
50g dark chocolate, chopped coarsely
⅔ cup (150g) caster sugar
⅓ cup (80ml) hot water
2 tablespoons coffee liqueur
1 tablespoon instant coffee granules
½ cup (75g) plain flour
1 tablespoon self-raising flour
1 tablespoon cocoa powder
1 egg, beaten lightly

1 Preheat oven to moderately slow (170°C/150°C fan-forced).
2 Follow method for Florentine cakes on page 37 for this cake.
3 Bake cake about 1¾ hours.

white wedding

This recipe makes three individual mini wedding cakes. Arrange the three together at different heights or levels (maybe even interwined with flowers) for a lovely effect.

White chocolate and apricot mud cake

125g butter, chopped coarsely
75g white chocolate, chopped coarsely
1 cup (220g) caster sugar
½ cup (125ml) milk
¾ cup (105g) plain flour
½ cup (75g) self-raising flour
½ cup (75g) finely chopped dried apricots
½ teaspoon vanilla extract
1 egg
⅓ cup (110g) apricot jam, warmed, strained
½ cup (80g) icing sugar
900g white prepared fondant

Modelling fondant

2 teaspoons gelatine
1½ tablespoons water
2 teaspoons glucose syrup
1½ cups (240g) pure icing sugar
½ cup (80g) pure icing sugar, extra

Royal icing

1½ cups (240g) pure icing sugar
1 egg white
½ teaspoon lemon juice

1 Make modelling fondant. On a surface dusted with extra icing sugar, roll fondant to approximately 3mm thick. Cut out flowers using 3.5cm and 1.5cm cutters (see page 105). Shape flowers using a ball tool (see pages 110 and 105); dry on tea towel.
2 Preheat oven to moderately slow (170°C/150°C fan-forced). Line 6-hole texas muffin pan with paper cases.
3 Combine butter, chocolate, sugar and milk in small saucepan; stir over low heat, until smooth. Transfer mixture to medium bowl; cool 15 minutes.
4 Whisk in sifted flours, apricots, then extract and egg; divide mixture among cases.
5 Bake cakes about 45 minutes. Turn cakes onto wire rack to cool.
6 Meanwhile make royal icing. Spoon icing into piping bag fitted with small plain tube, keep icing covered with a damp cloth.
7 Remove cases from cakes. Trim cake edges to make neat cylindrical shapes when stacked. Join two trimmed cakes with apricot jam; brush cakes all over with remaining jam.

8 On surface dusted with sifted icing sugar, knead fondant until smooth. Divide fondant into three equal portions. Roll out each portion to a thickness of 5mm. Cover the three cake stacks individually with fondant. Trim bases and smooth fondant (see page 110).
9 Pipe a little royal icing onto the back of each flower; secure to cake. Pipe some dots in the centre of each flower and around the base of each cake.

Modelling fondant

Sprinkle gelatine over the water in cup; stand cup in small saucepan of simmering water, stirring until gelatine is dissolved; add glucose. Place half the sifted icing sugar in medium bowl, stir in gelatine mixture. Gradually stir in remaining sifted icing sugar. Knead on surface dusted with extra sifted icing sugar until smooth. Wrap tightly in plastic wrap to prevent drying out.

Royal icing

Sift icing sugar through very fine sieve. Lightly beat egg white in small bowl with electric mixer; add icing sugar, a tablespoon at a time. When icing reaches firm peaks, use a wooden spoon to beat in juice; cover tightly with plastic wrap.

lily wedding cakes

Rich fruit cake
90g butter, softened
½ cup (110g) firmly packed
  brown sugar
2 eggs
1 tablespoon orange marmalade
500g (2¾ cups) mixed dried fruit,
  chopped finely
⅔ cup (100g) plain flour
2 tablespoons self-raising flour
1 teaspoon mixed spice
2 tablespoons sweet sherry
2 tablespoons sweet sherry, extra

Modelling fondant
2 teaspoons gelatine
1½ tablespoons water
2 teaspoons glucose syrup
1½ cups (240g) pure icing sugar
½ cup (80g) pure icing sugar, extra

Royal icing
1½ cups (240g) pure icing sugar
1 egg white
½ teaspoon lemon juice

Decorations
⅓ cup (110g) apricot jam,
  warmed, strained
½ cup (80g) icing sugar
900g white prepared fondant
covered 22 gauge wire
florist tape
30 stamens

1 Make modelling fondant. On surface dusted with extra sifted icing sugar, roll a little of the fondant to approximately 2mm thick. Cut out petals using lily petal cutter (see pages 105 and 111) allowing 6 petals for each cake. Vary size of petals to suit size of cakes. Using frilling tool (see pages 105 and 111), gently shape petals; attach damp 10cm length wire to each petal (see pages 105 and 111); allow to dry (see page 111).
2 Preheat oven to slow (150°C/ 130°C fan-forced). Line 6-hole texas or 12-hole standard muffin pan with paper cases.
3 Beat butter, sugar and eggs in small bowl with electric mixer until just combined.
4 Transfer mixture to medium bowl; add marmalade and fruit, mix well.
5 Sift flours and spice over mixture; add sherry, mix well. Divide mixture among cases; smooth surface.
6 Bake large cakes about 1 hour, small cakes about 50 minutes. Remove cakes from oven; brush tops with extra sherry. Cover pan tightly with foil; cool cakes in pan.
7 Meanwhile, assemble lilies using royal icing, stamens and pistles (see page 111).

8 Remove cases from cakes. Brush cakes with jam. On surface dusted with sifted icing sugar, knead prepared fondant until smooth. Divide fondant into six or 12 equal portions. Roll out each portion to a thickness of 5mm. Cover cakes with fondant; trim base and smooth fondant (see page 110).
9 Make royal icing. Spoon royal icing into piping bag fitted with small plain tube. Pipe a continuous line in a cornelli pattern over cakes (see page 112). Secure lilies to cakes.

Modelling fondant
Sprinkle gelatine over the water in cup; stand cup in small saucepan of simmering water, stirring until gelatine is dissolved, add glucose. Sift half the icing sugar in medium bowl, stir in gelatine mixture. Gradually stir in remaining sifted icing sugar, knead on surface dusted with extra sifted icing sugar until smooth. Wrap tightly in plastic wrap to prevent drying out.

Royal icing
Sift icing sugar through very fine sieve. Lightly beat egg white in small bowl; add icing sugar, a tablespoon at a time, beating well after each addition. When icing reaches firm peaks, add juice; beat well. Cover tightly with plastic wrap.

If your oven won't hold three sets of muffin pans, it's fine to leave the mixture standing at room temperature while the first batch bakes. We used three cake stands stacked on top of each other to display the cakes. They measured 17cm, 24cm and 34cm in diameter. We used a plastic filigree textured plate to mark the icing, available from craft or haberdashery shops. Mix and match the colours of the plates, cakes and flowers to suit the occasion.

Rich fruit cake

250g butter, softened
1¼ cups (250g) firmly packed brown sugar
4 eggs
2 tablespoons orange marmalade
1.5kg (7¾ cups) mixed dried fruit, chopped finely
1½ cups (225g) plain flour
½ cup (75g) self-raising flour
2 teaspoons mixed spice
½ cup (125ml) sweet sherry
¼ cup (30g) blanched whole almonds
2 tablespoons sweet sherry, extra

Decorations

½ cup (80g) icing sugar
750g white prepared fondant
filigree textured plate
½ cup (160g) orange marmalade, warmed, strained
silver lustre

1 Preheat oven to slow (150°C/130°C fan-forced). Line three 12-hole standard muffin pans with silver foil and paper cases.
2 Beat butter, sugar and eggs in small bowl with electric mixer until just combined.
3 Transfer mixture to large bowl, add marmalade and fruit; mix well.
4 Sift flours and spice over mixture, add sherry; mix well.
5 Place 2 level tablespoons of mixture into cases; smooth surface.
6 Bake cakes about 50 minutes. Remove cakes from oven; brush tops with extra sherry. Cover pan tightly with foil; cool cakes in pan.
7 On surface dusted with sifted icing sugar, knead fondant until smooth. Roll out to a thickness of 5mm. Using a 7cm round fluted cutter cut out 36 rounds.
8 Using a filigree textured plate (see page 105), gently press an imprint onto each fondant round (see page 115).
9 Brush cakes with marmalade; top with fondant rounds. Carefully brush silver lustre over pattern on fondant.

lace wedding cakes

deluxe chocolate wedding

You need to buy triple the quantity of the ingredients for the cake recipe below. You will need to make three separate batches, do not double or triple this recipe. It's important to measure the cake mixture carefully so the cakes are all the same depth. The mixture will be fine standing at room temperature while you bake the cakes in batches. Each batch will make 40 cakes. You need 120 standard muffin paper cases.

Mocha mud cake

500g butter, chopped coarsely
300g dark eating chocolate, chopped coarsely
4 cups (880g) caster sugar
2 cups (500ml) water
⅔ cup (160ml) coffee liqueur
2 tablespoons instant coffee granules
3 cups (450g) plain flour
½ cup (75g) self-raising flour
½ cup (50g) cocoa powder
4 eggs

Dark chocolate ganache

600ml thickened cream
800g dark eating chocolate, chopped coarsely

Decorations

15cm, 20cm, 30cm, 35cm and 45cm round boards
5m x 1.5cm cotton lace ribbon
4 empty cans, 9cm tall and 5cm in diameter
wrapping paper, for cans
200g milk eating chocolate
½ cup (115g) finely chopped glacé ginger
½ cup (10g) dried rose petals
¼ cup (25g) roasted coffee beans
2 miniature brandy snaps

1 Preheat oven to moderately slow (170°C/150°C fan-forced). Line two 12-hole standard muffin pans with paper cases.
2 Combine butter, chocolate, sugar, the water, liqueur and coffee in large saucepan; stir over low heat until smooth. Transfer mixture to large bowl; cool 15 minutes.

3 Whisk in sifted flours and cocoa, then eggs. Pour exactly ¼ cup of mixture into each case.
4 Bake cakes about 40 minutes. Turn cakes onto wire racks to cool.
5 Make dark chocolate ganache.
6 Attach ribbon to edge of round boards, using double sided tape. Cover cans with wrapping paper. Glue cans to centre of the four largest boards. Stack boards from the bottom tier up, as shown in picture.
7 Spread all cakes with ganache. Decorate cakes as shown with chocolate curls using vegetable peeler (see page 106), glacé ginger, coffee beans, rose petals and brandy snaps.
8 Place cakes on boards.

Dark chocolate ganache
Bring cream to a boil in medium saucepan, pour over chocolate in large bowl; stir until smooth. Cover bowl; refrigerate, about 30 minutes or until ganache is of a spreadable consistency.

toffee tumbles

Almond buttercake

150g butter, softened
½ teaspoon almond essence
⅔ cup (150g) caster sugar
2 eggs
⅓ cup (50g) self-raising flour
½ cup (75g) plain flour
½ cup (60g) almond meal

Choux pastry

60g butter
¾ cup (180ml) water
¾ cup (105g) plain flour
3 eggs, beaten lightly

Vanilla custard

1¼ cups (310ml) milk
1 vanilla bean, split
4 egg yolks
½ cup (110g) caster sugar
¼ cup (40g) cornflour

Toffee

1 cup (220g) caster sugar
½ cup (125ml) water

1 Make choux pastry; make vanilla custard.
2 Preheat oven to moderate (180°C/160°C fan-forced). Line 6-hole texas muffin or 12-hole standard pan with paper cases.
3 Beat butter, essence, sugar and eggs in small bowl with electric mixer until light and fluffy.
4 Stir in sifted flours and almond meal, in two batches. Divide mixture among cases; smooth surface.
5 Bake large cakes about 30 minutes, small cakes about 20 minutes. Turn cakes onto wire rack to cool.
6 Cut a 2cm deep hole in the centre of each cake, fill with custard; replace lid.
7 Spread tops of cakes with a little more custard. Top with a layer of puffs. Stack remaining puffs on cakes dipping each in a little custard.
8 Make toffee; drizzle over puffs.

Choux pastry

Preheat oven to hot (220°C/200°C fan-forced). Grease oven trays, line with baking paper. Combine butter with the water in medium saucepan; bring to a boil. Add flour; beat with wooden spoon over heat until mixture forms a smooth ball. Transfer mixture to small bowl; beat in egg with electric mixer in about six batches until mixture becomes glossy. Spoon mixture into piping bag fitted with 1cm plain tube. Pipe about 300 tiny dollops of pastry (about ¼ level teaspoon) 2cm apart, onto trays (see page 112); bake 7 minutes. Reduce oven to moderate (180°C/160°C fan-forced); bake for further 5 minutes or until puffs are crisp. Repeat with remaining mixture.

Vanilla custard

Bring milk and vanilla bean to a boil in small saucepan; discard vanilla bean. Meanwhile, beat egg yolks, sugar and cornflour in small bowl with electric mixer until thick. With motor operating, gradually beat in warm milk. Return custard to same pan; stir over heat until mixture boils and thickens. Cover surface of custard with plastic wrap; cool.

Toffee

Combine sugar with the water in small heavy-based saucepan. Stir over heat, without boiling, until sugar dissolves; bring to a boil. Reduce heat; simmer, uncovered, without stirring, until mixture is golden brown. Remove from heat; stand until bubbles subside before using.

apple custard tea cakes

Apple custard tea cakes
90g butter
½ teaspoon vanilla extract
½ cup (110g) caster sugar
2 eggs
¾ cup (110g) self-raising flour
¼ cup (30g) custard powder
2 tablespoons milk
1 large (200g) unpeeled apple, cored, sliced finely
30g butter, extra, melted
1 tablespoon caster sugar, extra
½ teaspoon ground cinnamon

Custard
1 tablespoon custard powder
1 tablespoon caster sugar
½ cup (125ml) milk
¼ teaspoon vanilla extract

1 Make custard.
2 Preheat oven to moderate (180°C/160°C fan-forced). Line 6-hole texas or 12-hole standard muffin pan with paper cases.
3 Beat butter, extract, sugar, eggs, flour, custard powder and milk in small bowl with electric mixer on low speed until ingredients are just combined. Increase speed to medium, beat until mixture is changed to a paler colour.
4 Divide half the mixture among cases. Top with custard, then remaining cake mixture; spread mixture to cover custard. Top with apple slices, pressing slightly into cake.
5 Bake large cakes about 40 minutes, small cakes about 30 minutes.
6 Brush hot cakes with extra butter, then sprinkle with combined extra sugar and cinnamon. Turn cakes onto wire rack. Serve warm or cold.

Custard
Blend custard powder and sugar with milk and extract in small saucepan; stir over heat until mixture boils and thickens. Remove from heat; cover surface with plastic wrap; cool.

We used green, orange and yellow paper muffin cases to match the decorations of these lovely cakes.

Poppy seed citrus cake

¼ cup (40g) poppy seeds
2 tablespoons milk
125g butter, softened
1 teaspoon finely grated lemon rind
1 teaspoon finely grated lime rind
⅔ cup (150g) caster sugar
2 eggs
1 cup (150g) self-raising flour
⅓ cup (50g) plain flour
⅓ cup (40g) almond meal
¼ cup (60ml) orange juice

Decorations

½ cup (80g) icing sugar
450g white prepared fondant
green, orange and yellow food colouring
⅓ cup (110g) orange marmalade, warmed, strained
2 tablespoons green sprinkles
2 tablespoons orange sprinkles
2 tablespoons yellow sprinkles

1 Preheat oven to moderate (180°C/160°C fan-forced). Line 6-hole texas or 12-hole standard muffin pan with paper cases.
2 Combine seeds and milk in small bowl; stand 20 minutes.
3 Beat butter, rinds, sugar and eggs in small bowl with electric mixer until light and fluffy.
4 Stir in sifted flours, almond meal, juice and poppy seed mixture. Divide mixture among cases; smooth surface.
5 Bake large cakes about 30 minutes, small cakes about 20 minutes. Turn cakes onto wire rack to cool.
6 On surface dusted with sifted icing sugar, knead fondant until smooth. Reserve 100g of fondant; enclose in plastic wrap. Divide remaining fondant into three equal portions; tint green, orange and yellow by kneading in colouring (see page 110). Wrap separately in plastic wrap.
7 Roll each of the coloured portions to a thickness of 5mm. Cut out rounds large enough to cover tops of cakes. Brush tops of cakes with marmalade, position rounds on cakes.
8 Roll reserved fondant into very thin lengths, cut off small pieces to represent seeds. Position lengths on top of cakes, using a little water, to represent segments.
9 Fill segments with matching coloured sprinkles; position fondant seeds.

100g dark chocolate Melts,
  melted
⅓ cup (110g) chocolate
  hazelnut spread
¼ cup (25g) hazelnut meal
1 tablespoon finely crushed
  ice cream wafer or cone
12 hazelnuts, toasted
1 tablespoon hazelnut meal,
  extra

1 Using small, clean paint brush,
paint chocolate thickly inside
twelve 2.5cm foil cases. Place
cases on tray; refrigerate about
5 minutes or until chocolate sets.
Peel away cases (see pages 106
and 107).
2 Combine spread and hazelnut
meal in small bowl; spoon mixture
into piping bag fitted with 1.5cm
fluted tube.
3 Divide pieces of wafer and
hazelnuts among cases. Pipe
chocolate mixture into cases.
Sprinkle with extra hazelnut meal.

chocolate hazelnut cups

Cherry chocolate mud cake

425g can pitted cherries in syrup
165g butter, chopped coarsely
100g dark eating chocolate,
    chopped coarsely
1⅓ cups (295g) caster sugar
¼ cup (60ml) cherry brandy
1 cup (150g) plain flour
2 tablespoons self-raising flour
2 tablespoons cocoa powder
1 egg

Decorations

⅔ cup (160ml) thickened cream,
    whipped
2 teaspoons cherry brandy
100g dark eating chocolate

black forest cakes

1 Preheat oven to moderately slow (170°C/150°C fan-forced). Line 6-hole texas or 12-hole standard muffin pan with paper cases.

2 Drain cherries; reserve syrup. Process ½ cup (110g) cherries with ½ cup (125ml) of the syrup until smooth. Halve remaining cherries; reserve for decorating cakes. Discard remaining syrup.

3 Combine butter, chocolate, sugar, brandy and cherry puree in small saucepan; stir over low heat until chocolate is melted. Transfer mixture to medium bowl; cool 15 minutes.

4 Whisk in sifted flours and cocoa, then egg. Divide mixture among cases; smooth surface.

5 Bake large cakes about 55 minutes, small cakes about 45 minutes. Turn cakes onto wire rack to cool.

6 Top cakes with remaining cherry halves and combined cream and cherry brandy. Using a vegetable peeler, make small chocolate curls (see page 106); sprinkle over cakes.

sweet violet cakes

Lemon cream cheese cake
90g butter, softened
90g cream cheese, softened
2 teaspoons finely grated
    lemon rind
⅔ cup (150g) caster sugar
2 eggs
⅓ cup (50g) self-raising flour
½ cup (75g) plain flour

Lemon cream cheese frosting
30g butter, softened
80g cream cheese, softened
1 teaspoon finely grated
    lemon rind
1½ cups (240g) icing sugar

Decorations
tea-lights
fresh violets

1 Preheat oven to moderate (180°C/160°C fan-forced). Line 6-hole texas or 12-hole standard muffin pan with paper cases.
2 Beat butter, cheese, rind, sugar and eggs in small bowl with electric mixer until light and fluffy.
3 Add sifted flours; beat on low speed until just combined. Divide mixture among cases; smooth surface.
4 Bake large cakes about 35 minutes, small cakes about 25 minutes. Turn cakes onto wire rack to cool.
5 Make lemon cream cheese frosting. Spread cakes with frosting; decorate with tea-lights and violets.

Lemon cream cheese frosting
Beat butter, cream cheese and rind in small bowl with electric mixer until light and fluffy; gradually beat in sifted icing sugar.

pineapple hibiscus cakes

Pineapple carrot cake

½ cup (125ml) vegetable oil
3 eggs, beaten lightly
1½ cups (225g) self-raising flour
¾ cup (165g) caster sugar
½ teaspoon ground cinnamon
2 cups (440g) firmly packed
  coarsely grated carrot
¾ cup (160g) drained crushed
  pineapple

Pineapple flowers

1 tablespoon caster sugar
1 tablespoon water
12 wafer thin slices fresh
  pineapple

Lemon cream cheese frosting

30g butter, softened
80g cream cheese, softened
1 teaspoon finely grated
  lemon rind
1½ cups (240g) icing sugar

1 Make pineapple flowers.
2 Preheat oven to moderate
(180°C/160°C fan-forced). Line a
6-hole texas or 12-hole standard
muffin pan with paper cases.
3 Combine oil, eggs, flour, sugar
and cinnamon in medium bowl;
stir until combined. Stir in carrot
and pineapple.
4 Divide mixture among cases.
5 Bake large cakes about
40 minutes, small cakes about
30 minutes. Turn cakes onto
wire rack to cool.
6 Make lemon cream cheese
frosting; spread on top of cakes.
Decorate with pineapple flowers.

Pineapple flowers

Preheat oven to very slow
(120°C/100°C fan-forced). Stir
sugar and the water together in
a small saucepan over low heat
until sugar has dissolved; boil
1 minute. Brush both sides of
pineapple slices with sugar syrup.
Place slices in a single layer on
wire racks over oven trays (see
page 115). Dry pineapple in oven
for about 1 hour. Immediately
remove slices from rack; carefully
shape into flowers. Dry over an
egg carton (see page 115).

Lemon cream cheese frosting

Beat butter, cream cheese and
rind in small bowl with electric
mixer until light and fluffy;
gradually beat in sifted icing sugar.

passionfruit curd cakes

Passionfruit buttercake
90g butter, softened
½ cup (110g) caster sugar
2 eggs
1 cup (150g) self-raising flour
¼ cup (60ml) passionfruit pulp

Passionfruit curd
2 eggs, beaten lightly
⅓ cup caster sugar
1 tablespoon lemon juice
¼ cup passionfruit pulp
60g butter, chopped coarsely

Decorations
85g packet passionfruit jelly
1 cup (250ml) boiling water
1 cup (80g) desiccated coconut
½ cup (125ml) thickened cream,
  whipped

1 Make passionfruit curd.
2 Preheat oven to moderate (180°C/160°C fan-forced). Line 6-hole texas or 12-hole standard muffin pan with paper cases.
3 Beat butter, sugar, eggs and flour in small bowl with electric mixer on low speed until ingredients are just combined. Increase speed to medium, beat until mixture is changed to a paler colour. Stir in passionfruit pulp.
4 Divide mixture among cases; smooth surface.
5 Bake large cakes about 25 minutes, small cakes about 20 minutes. Turn cakes onto wire rack to cool.
6 Dissolve jelly in the water. Refrigerate about 30 minutes or until set to the consistency of unbeaten egg white.
7 Remove cases from cakes. Roll cakes in jelly; leave cakes to stand in jelly for 15 minutes turning occasionally. Roll cakes in coconut; place on wire rack over tray. Refrigerate 30 minutes.
8 Cut cakes in half; fill with curd and cream.

Passionfruit curd
Combine ingredients in a small heatproof bowl, place over a small saucepan of simmering water; stir constantly until mixture thickens slightly and coats the back of a spoon. Remove from heat. Cover tightly; refrigerate curd until cold.

chocolate ginger gum nuts

Chocolate ginger mud cake
165g butter, chopped coarsely
100g dark eating chocolate,
    chopped coarsely
1⅓ cups (295g) caster sugar
⅔ cup (160ml) green ginger wine
¼ cup (60ml) water
1 cup (150g) plain flour
2 tablespoons self-raising flour
2 tablespoons cocoa powder
1 egg
⅓ cup (75g) finely chopped
    glacé ginger

Chocolate decorations
100g dark chocolate Melts,
    melted
100g milk chocolate Melts,
    melted
fresh rose leaves, washed

Dark chocolate ganache
½ cup (125ml) thickened cream
200g dark eating chocolate,
    chopped coarsely

1 Make chocolate decorations
– gum nuts, branches and leaves.
2 Preheat oven to moderately slow
(170°C/150°C fan-forced). Line
6-hole texas or 12-hole standard
muffin pan with paper cases.
3 Combine butter, chocolate,
sugar, wine and the water in small
saucepan; stir over low heat until
smooth. Transfer to medium bowl;
cool 15 minutes.
4 Whisk in sifted flours and cocoa,
then egg. Stir in ginger. Divide
mixture among cases.
5 Bake large cakes about 1 hour,
small cakes about 50 minutes.
Turn cakes onto wire rack to cool.
6 Make dark chocolate ganache.
7 Pour ganache over cakes; set at
room temperature.
8 Decorate cakes with chocolate
gum nuts, branches and leaves.

Chocolate decorations
For gum nuts, spread dark
chocolate onto a cold surface;
when set, pull a melon baller over
chocolate to make gum nuts (see
page 106). For branches, spoon
half the milk chocolate into paper
piping bag (see page 107); pipe
branches onto a baking paper-
lined tray (see page 107); leave to
set. Gently lift branches off paper.
For leaves, using a small, clean
paint brush, paint remaining milk
chocolate thickly on one side of
each leaf (see page 106), place on
baking paper-lined tray; leave to
set. Carefully peel away and discard
leaves (see page 107).

Dark chocolate ganache
Bring cream to a boil in small
saucepan; pour over chocolate
in small bowl; stir until smooth.
Stand at room temperature
until ganache becomes a thick
pouring consistency.

no-bake chocolate cakes

5 x 60g Mars bars
50g butter
3½ cups (120g) Rice Bubbles
200g milk eating chocolate,
  melted

1 Line a 12-hole standard muffin pan with paper cases.
2 Chop four Mars bars coarsely; cut remaining bar into slices.
3 Place chopped bars in medium saucepan with butter; stir over low heat until smooth. Stir in Rice Bubbles.
4 Press mixture into cases, spread with chocolate; top with sliced Mars bar. Refrigerate 30 minutes or until set.

easter egg baskets

Light fruit cake

125g butter, softened
½ teaspoon almond essence
⅔ cup (150g) caster sugar
2 eggs
⅔ cup (140g) red and green
  glacé cherries, quartered
⅓ cup (55g) sultanas
½ cup (70g) slivered almonds
⅔ cup (100g) plain flour
⅓ cup (50g) self-raising flour
¼ cup (60ml) milk

Royal icing

3 cups (480g) pure icing sugar
2 egg whites
1 teaspoon lemon juice
brown food colouring

Decorations

300g sugared almonds or
  mini chocolate eggs

1 Preheat oven to moderately slow (170°C/150°C fan-forced). Line 6-hole texas or 12-hole standard muffin pan with paper cases.
2 Beat butter, essence, sugar and eggs in small bowl with electric mixer until light and fluffy.
3 Add fruit and nuts; mix well. Stir in sifted flours and milk. Divide mixture among cases; smooth surface.
4 Bake large cakes about 45 minutes, small cakes about 40 minutes. Turn cakes onto wire rack to cool.
5 Make royal icing.
6 Remove cases from cakes. Pipe basket weave around cakes (see page 113); leave to dry for 3 hours or overnight.
7 Fill baskets with sugared almonds or chocolate eggs.

Royal icing

Sift icing sugar through very fine sieve. Lightly beat egg whites in small bowl with electric mixer; beat in icing sugar, a tablespoon at a time. When icing reaches firm peaks, use wooden spoon to beat in juice and colouring; cover tightly with plastic wrap.

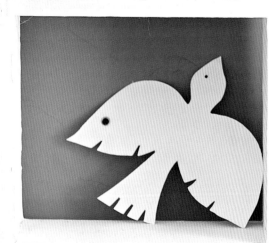

spicy christmas cakes

Make these festive cupcakes for Christmas; serve warm with brandy butter, whipped cream or custard.

Buttermilk spice cake
½ cup (110g) firmly packed brown sugar
½ cup (75g) plain flour
½ cup (75g) self-raising flour
¼ teaspoon bicarbonate of soda
1 teaspoon ground ginger
½ teaspoon ground cinnamon
¼ teaspoon ground nutmeg
90g butter, softened
1 egg
¼ cup (60ml) buttermilk
2 tablespoons golden syrup

Christmas decorations
½ cup (80g) icing sugar
100g white prepared fondant
5cm lengths of covered 24 gauge wire

Filling
½ cup (180g) fruit mince
1 tablespoon icing sugar

1 Make Christmas decorations.
2 Preheat oven to moderate (180°C/160°C fan-forced). Line 6-hole texas or 12-hole standard muffin pan with paper cases.
3 Sift dry ingredients into small bowl, add remaining ingredients; beat with electric mixer on low speed until ingredients are combined. Increase speed to medium, beat until mixture is smooth and changed to a paler colour. Divide mixture among cases; smooth surface.
4 Bake large cakes about 35 minutes, small cakes about 25 minutes. Turn cakes onto wire rack to cool for 5 minutes.
5 Cut a 2cm deep hole in the centre of each warm cake; discard cake rounds. Fill centres with fruit mince mixture. Top with wired fondant shapes; dust with a little sifted icing sugar.

Christmas decorations
On surface dusted with sifted icing sugar, knead fondant until smooth. Roll out to 1cm thickness. Cut out fondant shapes using Christmas cutters (see page 105). Insert a length of damp wire into each shape. Dry overnight on baking paper-lined tray.

Filling
Warm fruit mince in small saucepan over low heat; stir in icing sugar. Or, heat fruit mince in a microwave oven for about 30 seconds on HIGH (100%); stir in icing sugar.

christmas tree cakes

125g butter, softened
1 teaspoon coconut essence
⅔ cup (150g) caster sugar
2 eggs
1 cup (180g) finely chopped
   dried tropical fruit salad
½ cup (75g) macadamia nuts,
   chopped coarsely
⅔ cup (100g) plain flour
⅓ cup (50g) self-raising flour
⅓ cup (25g) desiccated coconut
¼ cup (60ml) milk

Coconut ice frosting
2 egg whites
1 teaspoon coconut essence
1½ cups (240g) icing sugar
1 cup (90g) desiccated coconut

Decorations
10 star fruit, approximately
green edible glitter

1 Preheat oven to moderately slow (170°C/150°C fan-forced). Line 6-hole texas or 12-hole standard muffin pan with paper cases.
2 Beat butter, essence, sugar and eggs in small bowl with electric mixer until light and fluffy.
3 Stir in dried fruit and nuts, then sifted flours, coconut and milk. Divide mixture among cases; smooth surface.
4 Bake large cakes about 45 minutes, small cakes about 35 minutes. Turn cakes onto wire racks to cool.
5 Make coconut ice frosting; top cakes with frosting.
6 Cut star fruit into 5mm slices. Arrange slices to make Christmas tree shapes of varying heights and sizes depending on size of cakes used. Use toothpicks or trimmed bamboo skewers to hold star fruit in position. Sprinkle with glitter.

Coconut ice frosting
Beat egg whites and essence in small bowl with electric mixer until foamy. Beat in sifted icing sugar in about four batches; stir in coconut.

christmas snowflakes

Rich fruit cake

90g butter, softened
½ cup (110g) firmly packed
    brown sugar
2 eggs
1 tablespoon orange marmalade
500g (2¾ cups) mixed dried fruit,
    chopped finely
⅔ cup (100g) plain flour
2 tablespoons self-raising flour
1 teaspoon mixed spice
2 tablespoons sweet sherry
2 tablespoons sweet sherry, extra

Decorations

½ cup (80g) icing sugar
300g white prepared fondant
½ teaspoon silver lustre
½ teaspoon vodka
silver cachous
⅓ cup (110g) apricot jam,
    warmed, strained

1 Preheat oven to slow (150°C/
130°C fan-forced). Line 6-hole
texas muffin or 12-hole standard
pan with paper cases.
2 Beat butter, sugar and eggs in
small bowl with electric mixer until
just combined.
3 Stir in marmalade and fruit;
mix well.
4 Sift flours and spice over
mixture; add sherry, mix well.
Divide mixture among cases;
smooth surface.
5 Bake large cakes about 1 hour,
small cakes about 50 minutes.
Remove cakes from oven; brush
tops with extra sherry. Cover pan
tightly with foil; cool cakes in pan.

6 On surface dusted with sifted
icing sugar, knead fondant until
smooth; roll out to a thickness
of 5mm. Using a fluted cutter,
cut out rounds large enough
to almost cover tops of cakes.
7 Using a cardboard snowflake
template (see page 105), gently
press an imprint into the centre of
each fondant round (see page 115).
8 Brush cakes with jam; top with
fondant rounds. Blend lustre with
vodka, paint onto snowflakes;
push silver cachous gently into
rounds.

jewelettes

Festive jewel cake

2 rings (55g) glacé pineapple
3 whole (85g) glacé apricots
1 cup (140g) seeded dried dates
⅔ cup (140g) red and green
  glacé cherries
½ cup (80g) whole blanched
  almonds
1 cup (160g) brazil nuts
2 eggs
⅓ cup (75g) firmly packed
  brown sugar
1 tablespoon dark rum
60g butter, softened
¼ cup (35g) plain flour
2 tablespoons self-raising flour

Topping

3 rings (80g) glacé pineapple
½ cup (100g) red and green
  glacé cherries, halved
½ cup (80g) brazil nuts
½ cup (80g) whole blanched
  almonds
⅓ cup (110g) apricot jam,
  warmed, strained

1 Preheat oven to slow
(150°C/130°C fan-forced). Line
6-hole texas or 12-hole standard
muffin pan with paper cases.
2 Coarsely chop pineapple and
apricots, halve cherries and nuts
for large cakes. Chop fruit and nuts
slightly smaller for small cakes.
3 Combine fruit and nuts in
medium bowl.
4 Beat eggs in small bowl with
electric mixer until thick and
creamy; add sugar, rum and
butter, beat until just combined.
5 Stir egg mixture into fruit
mixture with sifted flours. Divide
mixture among cases; press firmly
into cases.
6 Make topping; divide evenly
over cakes.
7 Bake large cakes about
1¼ hours, small cakes about
1 hour; cover cakes loosely with
foil halfway through baking time.
Cool cakes in pan.
8 Remove cakes from pan; brush
tops with jam.

Topping

Coarsely chop pineapple;
combine with remaining fruit
and nuts for large cakes. Chop
fruit and nuts slightly smaller for
small cakes. Combine fruit and
nuts in small bowl; mix well.

1. Piping bags
Available from cake decorating shops, chefs' supply shops and cookware shops, these are usually made from a waterproof fabric. Bags can also be made from baking or greaseproof paper; ideal for small amounts of icing (see page 107).

2. Rolling pins, brushes and metal spatulas
Mini rolling pins are available from cake decorating shops; fine artists' brushes from stationers, and metal spatulas from cookware shops.

3. Florist tape and wire
These are used to hold flowers and fondant shapes in position. Always cover wire or flower stems with florist tape if they are to be inserted into icing or cake.

4. Cutters
Come in all shapes and sizes; available from cake decorating or chefs' suppliers; these are usually made from metal or plastic.

5. Cake pans
Each recipe specifies the required muffin pan size – large, medium and small:
6-hole texas (¾ cup/180ml)
12-hole standard (⅓ cup/80ml)
12-hole mini (1 tablespoon/20ml)

6. Paper and foil cases
Each recipe specifies the required paper case size, this denotes the pan size. Measured across the base: texas muffin 6.5cm, freeform 6cm, standard muffin 5cm, mini muffin 3cm, foil cases 2.5cm. Paper cases are available from cake decorating shops, chefs' supply shops, supermarkets and cookware shops.

7. Lustre and edible colour
Is a powder available from cake decorating suppliers and craft shops in metallic shades, and is applied with a paintbrush. It is considered 'edible' in Europe and classified non-toxic for decoration only in Australia and the United States. Edible glitter is a non-metallic decoration for cakes.

8. Templates, lace and stamps
Templates and rubber stamps can be bought from cake decorating shops, craft shops and some stationers.

9. Colourings
Many types are available from cake decorating suppliers, craft shops and some supermarkets; all are concentrated. Use a minute amount of any type of colouring first to determine its strength. They are also available in liquid, gel, powder and paste forms. Powdered are edible and are used when primary colours or black are needed. Concentrated pastes are a little more expensive but are the easiest to use; are suitable for both pastel and stronger colours.

10. Flower making tools
A ball tool is used to shape petals and flowers; a frilling tool is used to shape lily petals; stamens are used for flower centres. These can all be bought from specialist cake decorating suppliers.

11. Icing tubes
Are made from metal or plastic, and can be bought from cake decorating suppliers, some craft shops, supermarkets and cookware shops.

Melting chocolate
Place coarsely chopped chocolate in small heatproof bowl, over small saucepan of simmering water; stir occasionally, until chocolate is melted. It is important that water not be allowed to come in contact with the chocolate, if it does it will sieze. You can melt chocolate in a microwave oven; melt on MEDIUM (55%) about 1 minute, stirring twice during melting.

Making small chocolate curls
Using a sharp vegetable peeler, scrape along the side of a long piece of room-temperature eating-quality chocolate. Clean the peeler often so that the chocolate doesn't clog the surface of the blade.

Making chocolate curls using melon baller
Spread melted chocolate evenly and thinly onto a piece of marble, laminated board or flat oven tray; stand at room temperature until just set but not hard. Pull a melon baller over the surface of chocolate to make curls. We used these as gum nuts (see page 103).

Painting foil cases & leaves with chocolate
Use a fine clean, dry paintbrush. Paint melted chocolate thickly inside each foil case or onto one side of a clean freshly-picked leaf; leave to set at room temperature.

Finishing chocolate foil cases & leaves

Carefully peel back case or leaf from chocolate. These can be made ahead and stored in an airtight container at room temperature until required. If the weather is hot, keep them in the refrigerator.

Colouring white chocolate

Using a skewer, add a few drops of colouring (the amount depends on the intensity of the colouring) into melted white chocolate and stir with a clean dry spoon, until colour is even. Too much colouring will cause chocolate to seize, that is, clump and turn an unappealing colour.

Making a piping bag

Cut a 30cm square of baking or greaseproof paper in half diagonally; hold apex of one triangle towards you. Twist first one point, then the other, into a cone shape. Bring three points together; secure the three points with a staple; repeat with other triangle. Sticky tape will hold a greaseproof bag together, but not one made from baking paper.

Piping chocolate

Place melted chocolate into paper piping bag. Snip end from bag. Cover an oven tray with baking paper, pipe desired shapes; leave to set at room temperature. Gently lift chocolate shapes from paper.

Making sugar syrup
Always place sugar and water in recommended size heavy-based saucepan. To prevent crystallisation or graininess, the sugar must be completely dissolved before the mixture boils. Stir constantly over medium to high heat to dissolve sugar. If sugar grains stick to the side of the pan, use a clean pastry brush dipped in water to brush down the sides of the pan.

Boiling sugar syrup
After sugar syrup comes to a boil, do not stir, and do not scrape pan or stir the syrup during cooking. Boil the syrup for about 5 minutes or until thick. Remove pan from heat; allow bubbles to subside before using. This stage can be measured accurately by buying a candy thermometer. The temperature should be 118°C. This stage is perfect for fluffy frosting.

Boiling sugar syrup to hard crack
Bring sugar syrup to a boil, reduce heat; simmer uncovered, without stirring for about 10 minutes or until mixture is golden. Remove from heat; stand until bubbles subside before using. If using a candy thermometer, mixture should be between 138°C and 154°C depending on the colour required. The longer the toffee boils and colours the harder it will set.

Candy thermometer
Thermometer should be stainless steel and have a clip to attach to the pan. Once sugar is dissolved, place thermometer in small saucepan of cold water (mercury must be covered). Bring the water to a boil, check thermometer for accuracy at boiling point. When sugar syrup comes to a boil, place thermometer in syrup (mercury must be covered). Boil to the required temperature. Return thermometer to pan of boiling water, remove from heat, allow thermometer to cool in the water.

Checking toffee for hard crack

To test toffee for hard crack use a clean dry spoon and carefully drizzle some toffee into cold water. If it has reached hard crack it should set immediately. Always remove the pan from the heat and allow the bubbles to subside before testing.

Testing toffee

Remove set toffee from cold water and snap between fingers. It should be brittle and snap easily.

Making toffee shards

When toffee reaches a golden colour, remove pan from heat, allow bubbles to subside; drizzle toffee from the back of a wooden spoon, onto a baking paper-lined oven tray. Allow toffee to set at room temperature. Remove shards from paper using a spatula. Immediately position on cake.

Shaping toffee over rolling pin

When toffee reaches a golden colour, remove pan from heat, allow bubbles to subside. Drizzle toffee from wooden spoon onto a rolling pin, covered with baking paper. Allow toffee to set at room temperature. Slide baking paper off rolling pin to remove toffee shapes. Immediately position on cake.

After kneading fondant until smooth, use a skewer to colour fondant; kneading colouring into fondant until desired colour is achieved. The amount of colouring needed will depend on the intensity of the colouring used.

Brush cakes lightly and evenly with jam. Roll almond paste or fondant to desired thickness; lift onto cake with hands or rolling pin. Smooth surface with hands dusted with icing sugar, ease paste or fondant around side and base of cake; trim excess with sharp knife.

Cut out flowers using cutter of choice, place flower on clean folded tea towel. Using ball tool, gently shape flower; leave to dry.

Roll out fondant to 2mm thick. Cut out wings, place damp wire into each wing; dry flat. Make body of butterfly by moulding a piece of fondant; attach wire to body.

Shaping butterfly
Bring wires, with wings attached, together. Use florist tape to secure wires and shape butterfly.

Making lily petals from modelling fondant
Knead fondant; roll to a thickness of 2mm. Using the lily petal cutter, cut out 6 petals for each flower. Frill along each edge, using thicker edge of frilling tool. Gently score two lines on each petal.

Drying lily petals
Dry individual petals in round-based patty pans or soup spoons. Bend the wire at a 90° angle from the petal.

Assembling lily
Wet one end of single wire lengths, insert into end of each petal; dry on baking paper-lined tray. For flower centre (pistle), roll tiny balls of fondant. Wet one end of single wire length, insert into balls; pinch balls several times with tweezers. To assemble lily, attach five stamens to pistle with florist tape. Attach one to two petals at a time, around pistle, using florist tape.

Piping choux pastry
Spoon choux pastry into piping bag fitted with a 1cm plain tube. Hold piping bag vertical to baking paper-lined oven tray; quickly pivot wrist, piping tiny dollops (equal to ¼ teaspoon) of choux pastry 2cm apart, onto tray.

Piping meringue
Spoon meringue into piping bag fitted with a 1cm plain tube. Hold piping bag vertical to the cake, piping a spiral from the outside to the centre of the cake.

Piping lines with royal icing
Spoon icing into piping bag fitted with a small plain tube. Gently touch surface with tip of tube, lightly squeezing piping bag. As icing comes out, lift tube up from surface, squeezing to desired length. Stop squeezing bag, placing icing down onto surface. Even pressure is paramount – too much will give uneven thickness, too little pressure and the line will break.

Piping cornelli pattern with royal icing
Spoon icing into piping bag fitted with a small plain tube. Hold tube tip close to cake surface so that icing attaches without tube scraping cake or flattening the icing line. Pipe a continuous, meandering line of icing; move tip up, around and down to produce a lacy effect – don't let lines touch or cross.

Piping basket weave with royal icing

Using a basket weave tube, pipe a long vertical line from the top of the cake to the bottom, followed by short horizontal lines across the long vertical line. The horizontal lines should be a tube-width apart.

Pipe the next long vertical line at the end of the previous short horizontal lines.

Pipe short horizontal lines into the gaps, between the two vertical lines.

Repeat previous steps, continuing the basket weave design until the design meets with the starting point.

Shaping cakes
Using a serrated knife carefully shave edges of cake away.

Sugar-frosting fruit
Using a small clean paint brush, lightly and sparingly brush fruit individually with egg white; dip wet fruit in sugar. Place frosted fruit on baking paper-lined tray. Leave about 1 hour or until sugar is dry.

Dusting-on designs
The best results are achieved by using several doilies still joined together, pieces of plastic backed lace tablecloths or thick fabric lace, as they are easier to lift away from the cake once dusted with icing sugar.

Feather and fan
Place chocolate topping into paper piping bag. Starting in the centre of the cream topped cake, pipe a spiral. Using a skewer, gently drag through the spiral design, from the cake centre to the edge of the paper case.

more techniques

Drying pears and pineapple

Fruit needs to be sliced thinly and evenly – a mandoline or V-slicer is ideal, alternatively use a very sharp knife. Using a clean pastry brush, brush both sides of sliced fruit with sugar syrup. Place fruit on wire rack over an oven tray. Bake for specified time.

Shaping dried pears and pineapple

Dried fruit slices must be lifted from wire rack immediately after baking to prevent sticking. For pear slices, shape by pinching narrow end; dry on wire rack. For pineapple slices, pinch centre of each slice; dry over egg carton.

Colouring sugar

Use granulated or caster sugar, depending on the texture you prefer. Place required amount of sugar in a plastic bag, add a tiny amount of colouring; work colouring through sugar by 'massaging' plastic bag. Sugar will keep in a jar at room temperature indefinitely.

Marking fondant

Roll fondant to desired thickness; place textured templates onto fondant, pressing gently to leave an imprint. Lift template away from fondant. Or, gently press cardboard stencil into fondant, leaving imprint. Paint imprint with colouring or fill with coloured sugar or sprinkles. Or, using a small, clean brush, paint design on stamp with coloured paste; gently press stamp onto fondant, to leave a coloured imprint.

glossary

after dinner mints mint squares coated in dark chocolate.

almonds
blanched brown skins removed.
flaked paper-thin slices.
meal also called ground almonds.
slivered small lengthways-cut pieces.

bicarbonate of soda also known as baking soda.

brandy snap is a crisp wafer thin sweet biscuit.

butter use salted or unsalted ('sweet') butter; 125g is equal to 1 stick of butter.

buttermilk sold in the refrigerated dairy compartments in supermarkets. It is the liquid left after cream is separated from milk.

cachous small, round cake-decorating sweets available in silver, gold and various colours.

chocolate
dark we used premium-quality dark eating chocolate, not compound.
melts discs made of milk, white or dark compound chocolate; good for melting and moulding.
milk primarily for eating.
topping also called chocolate sauce.
white eating chocolate.

chocolate hazelnut spread also known as Nutella.

cocoa powder also known as cocoa; dried, unsweetened, roasted ground cocoa beans.

coconut
desiccated unsweetened and concentrated, dried finely shredded.
flaked dried flaked coconut flesh.
liqueur we used Malibu.
shredded thin strips of dried coconut flesh.

coffee-flavoured liqueur we used either Tia Maria or Kahlua.

craisins dried cranberries.

cream, thickened a whipping cream containing thickener with a minimum fat content of 35%.

cream cheese commonly known as Philadelphia or Philly, it is a soft cow-milk cheese with fat content of at least 33%.

coloured sprinkles also known as Dollar Fives.

custard powder instant mixture used to make pouring custard; similar to North American instant pudding mixes.

dried mixed berries lightly crunchy dehydrated form of strawberries, blueberries and cherries. They can be eaten as is or used as an ingredient in cooking.

dried fruit salad commonly made with tropical fruit like paw paw, pineapple and mango.

eggs some recipes in this book call for raw or barely cooked eggs; exercise caution if there is a salmonella problem in your area.

essence a synthetically produced substance used sparingly to impart flavour to foods.

ferrero raffaello is a crispy, creamy almond and coconut bite-sized sweet. Available from supermarkets.

flour
cornflour also known as cornstarch.
plain an all-purpose flour, made from wheat.
self-raising plain (all purpose) flour sifted with baking powder in the proportion of 1 cup flour to 2 teaspoons baking powder.

fruit mince also called mince meat; a sweet mixture of dried fruits, sugar, suet, nuts and flavourings.

gelatine (gelatin) we used powdered gelatine as a setting agent.

ginger wine made with a grape base to which ginger, spices, herbs and fruits have been added.

glacé fruits fruits that have been cooked in heavy syrup.

glucose syrup also known as liquid glucose; a sugary syrup made from starches such as wheat and corn.

golden syrup a by-product of refined sugarcane.

hazelnut meal also called ground hazelnuts.

jam also called preserve or conserve.

maple-flavoured syrup made from sugar cane rather than maple-tree sap; used in cooking or as a topping but cannot be considered an exact substitute for pure maple syrup.

marmalade is a jam or conserve made with shredded citrus rind.

marsala a sweet fortified wine originally from Sicily.

Mars bar a chocolate-coated caramel confectionery bar.

mascarpone a fresh, thick, triple-cream cheese with a delicately sweet, slightly sour taste.

milk we used full-cream homogenised milk.

mixed dried fruit also known as dried fruit; commonly a combination of sultanas, raisins, currants, mixed peel and cherries.

mixed spice a blend of ground spices usually consisting of cinnamon, allspice and nutmeg.

plain sweet biscuits un-iced biscuits or cookies used to make crumbs.

poppy seeds possessing a nutty, slightly sweet flavour and a dark blue-grey colour, come from capsules inside an opium plant indigenous to the Mediterranean.

prepared fondant also known as soft icing and ready-to-roll.

Rice Bubbles also known as Rice Krispies, are made of rice and are an example of a puffed grain cereal.

rind also known as zest.

rose petals, dried slightly chewy, dehydrated form of this popular flower. They can be used to flavour sweet and savoury dishes.

rosewater extract made from crushed rose petals, called gulab in India; used for its aromatic quality in many sweetmeats and desserts.

sour cream thick, commercially-cultured with a minimum fat content of 35%.

star fruit also known as carambola, five-corner fruit or Chinese star fruit.

sugar
brown a soft, fine granulated sugar containing molasses to give its characteristic colour.

caster also known as superfine or finely granulated table sugar.
granulated table sugar, coarser than caster sugar.
icing also called confectioners' or powdered sugar; crushed granulated sugar with added cornflour (about 3%).
pure icing confectioners' sugar.
vanilla is granulated or caster sugar flavoured with a vanilla bean. Can be stored indefinitely.

sultanas also called golden raisins.

top 'n' fill a canned milk product made of condensed milk that has been boiled to a caramel.

vanilla
bean dried long, thin pod from a tropical golden orchid grown in Central and South America and Tahiti. Tiny black seeds inside the bean are used to impart a vanilla flavour in baking and desserts.
extract distilled from the seeds of the vanilla pod.

vegetable oil any of a number of oils sourced from plants rather than animal fats.

violet crumble a honeycomb bar coated in milk chocolate.

vodka clear, colourless, flavourless spirit that evaporates as it dries.

conversion chart

Measures

One Australian metric measuring cup holds approximately 250ml; one Australian metric tablespoon holds 20ml; one Australian metric teaspoon holds 5ml.

The difference between one country's measuring cups and another's is within a two- or three-teaspoon variance, and will not affect your cooking results. North America, New Zealand and the United Kingdom use a 15ml tablespoon.

All cup and spoon measurements are level. The most accurate way of measuring dry ingredients is to weigh them. When measuring liquids, use a clear glass or plastic jug with the metric markings.

We use large eggs with an average weight of 60g.

Dry measures

METRIC	IMPERIAL
15g	½oz
30g	1oz
60g	2oz
90g	3oz
125g	4oz (¼lb)
155g	5oz
185g	6oz
220g	7oz
250g	8oz (½lb)
280g	9oz
315g	10oz
345g	11oz
375g	12oz (¾lb)
410g	13oz
440g	14oz
470g	15oz
500g	16oz (1lb)
750g	24oz (1½lb)
1kg	32oz (2lb)

Liquid measures

METRIC	IMPERIAL
30ml	1 fluid oz
60ml	2 fluid oz
100ml	3 fluid oz
125ml	4 fluid oz
150ml	5 fluid oz (¼ pint/1 gill)
190ml	6 fluid oz
250ml	8 fluid oz
300ml	10 fluid oz (½ pint)
500ml	16 fluid oz
600ml	20 fluid oz (1 pint)
1000ml (1 litre)	1¾ pints

Length measures

3mm	⅛in
6mm	¼in
1cm	½in
2cm	¾in
2.5cm	1in
5cm	2in
6cm	2½in
8cm	3in
10cm	4in
13cm	5in
15cm	6in
18cm	7in
20cm	8in
23cm	9in
25cm	10in
28cm	11in
30cm	12in (1ft)

Oven temperatures

These oven temperatures are only a guide for conventional ovens. For fan-forced ovens, check the manufacturer's manual.

	°C (CELSIUS)	°F (FAHRENHEIT)	GAS MARK
Very slow	120	250	½
Slow	150	275-300	1-2
Moderately slow	170	325	3
Moderate	180	350-375	4-5
Moderately hot	200	400	6
Hot	220	425-450	7-8
Very hot	240	475	9

index

ACP BOOKS

General manager Christine Whiston
Editor-in-chief Susan Tomnay
Creative director Hieu Chi Nguyen
Art director Hannah Blackmore
Designer Lisa Cainero
Senior editor Stephanie Kistner
Food director Pamela Clark
Home economists Ariarne Bradshaw, Belinda Farlow, Nicole Jennings, Elizabeth Macri,
Angela Muscat, Kirrily DeRosa, Rebecca Squadrito, Kellie-Marie Thomas
Sales & rights director Brian Cearnes
Marketing manager Bridget Cody
Senior business analyst Rebecca Varela
Circulation manager Jama Mclean
Operations manager David Scotto
Production manager Victoria Jefferys

ACP Books are published by ACP Magazines a division of PBL Media Pty Limited
PBL Media, Chief Executive Officer Ian Law
Publishing & sales director, Women's lifestyle Lynette Phillips
Editor at Large, Women's lifestyle Pat Ingram
Marketing director, Women's lifestyle Matthew Dominello
Commercial manager, Women's lifestyle Seymour Cohen
Research director, Women's lifestyle Justin Stone

Produced by ACP Books, Sydney.

Published by ACP Books, a division of ACP Magazines Ltd, 54 Park St, Sydney; GPO Box 4088, Sydney, NSW 2001.
phone (02) 9282 8618; fax (02) 9267 9438. acpbooks@acpmagazines.com.au; www.acpbooks.com.au

Printed by Dai Nippon in Korea.

Australia Distributed by Network Services, phone +61 2 9282 8777; fax +61 2 9264 3278;
networkweb@networkservicescompany.com.au
United Kingdom Distributed by Australian Consolidated Press (UK), phone (01604) 642 200;
fax (01604) 642 300; books@acpuk.com
New Zealand Distributed by Netlink Distribution Company, phone (9) 366 9966; ask@ndc.co.nz
South Africa Distributed by PSD Promotions, phone (27 11) 392 6065/6/7;
fax (27 11) 392 6079/80; orders@psdprom.co.za
Canada Distributed by Publishers Group Canada
phone (800) 663 5714; fax (800) 565 3770; service@raincoast.com

Clark, Pamela.
The Australian women's weekly cupcakes and fairycakes.
Includes index.
ISBN: 978-1-86396-563-7
1. Cake. I. Title.
641.8653
© ACP Magazines Ltd 2006
ABN 18 053 273 546

The publishers would like to thank the following for props used in photography
Crave, Bellevue Hill; Iris & Hazel, Paddington; kikki. K, Bondi Junction; Mondo, Double Bay; My Island Home, Double Bay;
Orson & Blake, Woollahra; Pavillon Christofle, Double Bay; Signature Prints, Roseberry; Space Furniture, Alexandria;
Tatti, Double Bay; Top 3 By Design, Bondi Junction; Tres Fabu, Northbridge; T2, Chatswood; Iced Affair, Camperdown.

Send recipe enquiries to:
recipeenquiries@acpmagazines.com.au